It's Always Sunny and Philosophy

Popular Culture and Philosophy® Series Editor: George A. Reisch

VOLUME 1 *Seinfeld and Philosophy: A Book about Everything and Nothing* (2000)

VOLUME 2 *The Simpsons and Philosophy: The D'oh! of Homer* (2001)

VOLUME 3 *The Matrix and Philosophy: Welcome to the Desert of the Real* (2002)

VOLUME 4 *Buffy the Vampire Slayer and Philosophy: Fear and Trembling in Sunnydale* (2003)

VOLUME 9 *Harry Potter and Philosophy: If Aristotle Ran Hogwarts* (2004)

VOLUME 12 *Star Wars and Philosophy: More Powerful than You Can Possibly Imagine* (2005)

VOLUME 13 *Superheroes and Philosophy: Truth, Justice, and the Socratic Way* (2005)

VOLUME 19 *Monty Python and Philosophy: Nudge Nudge, Think Think!* (2006)

VOLUME 25 *The Beatles and Philosophy: Nothing You Can Think that Can't Be Thunk* (2006)

VOLUME 30 *Pink Floyd and Philosophy: Careful with that Axiom, Eugene!* (2007)

VOLUME 33 *Battlestar Galactica and Philosophy: Mission Accomplished or Mission Frakked Up?* (2008)

VOLUME 35 *Star Trek and Philosophy: The Wrath of Kant* (2008)

VOLUME 36 *The Legend of Zelda and Philosophy: I Link Therefore I Am* (2008)

VOLUME 39 *Jimmy Buffett and Philosophy: The Porpoise Driven Life* (2009) Edited by Erin McKenna and Scott L. Pratt

VOLUME 41 *Stephen Colbert and Philosophy: I Am Philosophy (And So Can You!)* (2009) Edited by Aaron Allen Schiller

VOLUME 42 *Supervillains and Philosophy: Sometimes, Evil Is Its Own Reward* (2009) Edited by Ben Dyer

VOLUME 44 *Led Zeppelin and Philosophy: All Will Be Revealed* (2009) Edited by Scott Calef

VOLUME 45 *World of Warcraft and Philosophy: Wrath of the Philosopher King* (2009) Edited by Luke Cuddy and John Nordlinger

Volume 46 *Mr. Monk and Philosophy: The Curious Case of the Defective Detective* (2010) Edited by D.E. Wittkower

Volume 47 *Anime and Philosophy: Wide Eyed Wonder* (2010) Edited by Josef Steiff and Tristan D. Tamplin

VOLUME 48 *The Red Sox and Philosophy: Green Monster Meditations* (2010) Edited by Michael Macomber

VOLUME 49 *Zombies, Vampires, and Philosophy: New Life for the Undead* (2010) Edited by Richard Greene and K. Silem Mohammad

VOLUME 51 *Soccer and Philosophy: Beautiful Thoughts on the Beautiful Game* (2010) Edited by Ted Richards

VOLUME 53 *Martial Arts and Philosophy: Beating and Nothingness* (2010) Edited by Graham Priest and Damon Young

VOLUME 54 *The Onion and Philosophy: Fake News Story True, Alleges Indignant Area Professor* (2010) Edited by Sharon M. Kaye

VOLUME 55 *Doctor Who and Philosophy: Bigger on the Inside* (2010) Edited by Courtland Lewis and Paula Smithka

VOLUME 56 *Dune and Philosophy: Weirding Way of the Mentat* (2011) Edited by Jeffery Nicholas

VOLUME 57 *Rush and Philosophy: Heart and Mind United* (2011) Edited by Jim Berti and Durrell Bowman

VOLUME 58 *Dexter and Philosophy: Mind over Spatter* (2011) Edited by Richard Greene, George A. Reisch, and Rachel Robison-Greene

VOLUME 59 *Halo and Philosophy: Intellect Evolved* (2011) Edited by Luke Cuddy

VOLUME 60 *SpongeBob SquarePants and Philosophy: Soaking Up Secrets Under the Sea!* (2011) Edited by Joseph J. Foy

VOLUME 61 *Sherlock Holmes and Philosphy: The Footprints of a Gigantic Mind* (2011) Edited by Josef Steiff

VOLUME 62 *Inception and Philosophy: Ideas to Die For* (2011) Edited by Thorsten Botz-Bornstein

VOLUME 63 *Philip K. Dick and Philosophy: Do Androids Have Kindred Spirits?* (2011) Edited by D.E. Wittkower

VOLUME 64 *The Rolling Stones and Philosophy: It's Just a Thought Away* (2012) Edited by Luke Dick and George A. Reisch

VOLUME 65 *Chuck Klosterman and Philosophy: The Real and the Cereal* (2012) Edited by Seth Vannatta

VOLUME 67 *Breaking Bad and Philosophy: Badder Living through Chemistry* (2012) Edited by David R. Koepsell and Robert Arp

VOLUME 68 *The Walking Dead and Philosophy: Zombie Apocalypse Now* (2012) Edited by Wayne Yuen

VOLUME 69 *Curb Your Enthusiasm and Philosophy: Awaken the Social Assassin Within* (2012) Edited by Mark Ralkowski

VOLUME 71 *The Catcher in the Rye and Philosophy: A Book for Bastards, Morons, and Madmen* (2012) Edited by Keith Dromm and Heather Salter

VOLUME 72 *Jeopardy! and Philosophy: What Is Knowledge in the Form of a Question?* (2012) Edited by Shaun P. Young

VOLUME 73 *The Wire and Philosophy: This America, Man* (2013) Edited by David Bzdak, Joanna Crosby, and Seth Vannatta

VOLUME 74 *Planet of the Apes and Philosophy: Great Apes Think Alike* (2013) Edited by John Huss

VOLUME 75 *Psych and Philosophy: Some Dark Juju-Magumbo* (2013) Edited by Robert Arp

VOLUME 77 *Boardwalk Empire and Philosophy: Bootleg This Book* (2013) Edited by Richard Greene and Rachel Robison-Greene

VOLUME 79 *Frankenstein and Philosophy: The Shocking Truth* (2013) Edited by Nicolas Michaud

VOLUME 80 *Ender's Game and Philosophy: Genocide Is Child's Play* (2013) Edited by D.E. Wittkower and Lucinda Rush

VOLUME 81 *How I Met Your Mother and Philosophy: Being and Awesomeness* (2014) Edited by Lorenzo von Matterhorn

VOLUME 82 *Jurassic Park and Philosophy: The Truth Is Terrifying* (2014) Edited by Nicolas Michaud and Jessica Watkins

VOLUME 83 *The Devil and Philosophy: The Nature of His Game* (2014) Edited by Robert Arp

VOLUME 84 *Leonard Cohen and Philosophy: Various Positions* (2014) Edited by Jason Holt

VOLUME 85 *Homeland and Philosophy: For Your Minds Only* (2014) Edited by Robert Arp

VOLUME 86 *Girls and Philosophy: This Book Isn't a Metaphor for Anything* (2014) Edited by Richard Greene and Rachel Robison-Greene

VOLUME 87 *Adventure Time and Philosophy: The Handbook for Heroes* (2014) Edited by Nicolas Michaud

VOLUME 88 *Justified and Philosophy: Shoot First, Think Later* (2014) Edited by Rod Carveth and Robert Arp

VOLUME 89 *Steve Jobs and Philosophy: For Those Who Think Different* (2015) Edited by Shawn E. Klein

VOLUME 90 *Dracula and Philosophy: Dying to Know* (2015) Edited by Nicolas Michaud

VOLUME 91 *It's Always Sunny and Philosophy: The Gang Gets Analyzed* (2015) Edited by Roger Hunt and Robert Arp

IN PREPARATION:

Orange Is the New Black and Philosophy (2015) Edited by Richard Greene and Rachel Robison-Greene

More Doctor Who and Philosophy (2015) Edited by Paula Smithka and Courtland Lewis

Divergent and Philosophy (2015) Edited by Courtland Lewis

Downton Abbey and Philosophy (2015) Edited by Adam Barkman and Robert Arp

Hannibal Lecter and Philosophy (2015) Edited by Joseph Westfall

The Princess Bride and Philosophy (2015) Edited by Richard Greene and Rachel Robison-Greene

The Ultimate Walking Dead and Philosophy (2015) Edited by Wayne Yuen

Louis C.K. and Philosophy (2015) Edited by Mark Ralkowski

Perry Mason and Philosophy (2016) Edited by Heather Rivera and Robert Arp

For full details of all Popular Culture and Philosophy® books, visit www.opencourtbooks.com.

Popular Culture and Philosophy®

It's Always Sunny and Philosophy

The Gang Gets Analyzed

Edited by

ROGER HUNT AND ROBERT ARP

OPEN COURT
Chicago

Volume 91 in the series, Popular Culture and Philosophy ®, edited by George A. Reisch

To order books from Open Court, call toll-free 1-800-815-2280, or visit our website at www.opencourtbooks.com.

Open Court Publishing Company is a division of Carus Publishing Company, dba Cricket Media.

ISBN: 978-0-8126-9891-6

Library of Congress Control Number: 2015012252

Contents

The Pataphysical?   vii

I Good   1

1. The Ancient Art of Being an Asshole
   GREG LITTMANN   3

2. No Restrictions, Baby!
   JASON IULIANO   21

3. Charlie Gets Beatified
   CHRISTOPHER KETCHAM   31

II Psychology   43

4. What's So Creepy about Unibrows and Incest?
   CHARLENE ELSBY   45

5. Psychoanalyzing the Game of Games
   DANIEL LEONARD   55

6. Are the Gang Authentic?
   CHARLOTTE KNOWLES   65

III Virtue   77

7. The Gang's Quest for Happiness—One Day at
   a Time
   KYLE ALKEMA AND ADAM BARKMAN   79

8. Frank Reynolds, Role Model
   ADAM HENSCHKE   91

9. The D.E.N.N.I.S System
   ROGER HUNT   103

Contents

IV Morals   111

10. Yes Means Yes, Unless It Means No
    TIM AYLSWORTH   113

11. The Gang Gets Pardoned
    ETHAN CHAMBERS   123

12. Ethics for Jabronis
    SKYLER KING   133

V Truth   145

13. The Gang's Crooked Thinking
    FENNER TANSWELL   147

14. Why Science Is a Liar Sometimes
    RUSS HAMER   159

15. The Gang Solves the Gas Crisis as a
    Nietzschean Parable
    MARTYN JONES   167

A Gallery of Real-Life Scumbags   179

Bitches, It's the Authors in the Book, Bitches   217

Index   221

The Pataphysical?

In "Flowers for Charlie," being under the influence of a placebo drug administered by scientists examining how believing in one's own intelligence can lead to becoming a pompous ass, Charlie decrees that he's exploring "the physical, the metaphysical, and the pataphysical." As we come to find out, he's hardly doing anything of those things, but we'd challenge anyone to watch that episode and honestly say they didn't believe for at least a second that Charlie had actually taken a cognitive enhancing drug and that he had actually become one of the most brilliant persons on the planet—he even got the Waitress to fall for him . . . finally!

Still, while fun plot lines like the one above have at least a hint of intellectual brilliance about them, as many *It's Always Sunny* episodes do, we'd venture a guess that many viewers won't consider *It's Always Sunny* to be philosophical. After all, most of the jokes are crude, misogynistic, and garner merely cheap laughs. But we like to think, and such thinking led to this volume, that there is something physically, metaphysically, and even pataphysically interesting about *It's Always Sunny*, though we think we have to get a bit meta to see it.

So, as crude as the following question sounds and as relentlessly asked and poked fun at and answered by people way smarter than me, we're going to ask it anyway: What is philosophy?

"Flowers for Charlie" is a good place to start, as it shows us what philosophy is not! Obviously Charlie himself wasn't being philosophical in this episode, but he was able to fool us, well at least us, that he was. So what was it that made Charlie seem philosophical?

For one, he used big, fancy-sounding words. We have known for a while that simply sounding smart isn't necessarily being smart, and in some cases people will try to sound smart simply because they have very little to say in the first place. This trait isn't simply limited to the intellectually vain, but also to those who are employed as philosophers. Several years back in a very fun, somewhat brutal experiment, a philosopher asked for submissions to a "Bad Writing Contest." Scholars were asked to find the most pompous, unintelligible passages from leading academic journals, and there would be an informal judging party to determine just which passages were the most heinous. Along these same lines, another scholar submitted a completely nonsensical paper to a leading academic journal, which published it, only to have the scholar later reveal that he made the whole thing up using words the scholars of the journal would like to hear, rather than based on any kind of philosophical or scientific reasoning.

Using fancy words obviously isn't philosophy.

And, of course, we all know people who like to use words to sound impressive, so that it happens in academic circles as well probably isn't much of a surprise. But since such posturing certainly only demonstrates that the person using the words is somehow deluded, it isn't really that interesting to discount as a condition for being philosophical since it only reflects poorly on the person using the words.

Another part of the ruse is slightly more damning: not only does the person using the words look silly, but all the people who believe the person using the words also look silly. Charlie seems to command the attention of what we can only understand to be leading researchers in the field. This kind of Guru Effect is somewhat more complex than simply using big words, because it means that not only are the words meaningless, but also that the people listening to them are believing and respecting something meaningless. Something isn't philosophical because a lot of people—maybe even other highly respected persons—believe it to be so.

Still, these points may not be entirely interesting. There's something *very* interesting, however, about this episode. Much of what Charlie says—especially in regard to the waitress—*is* true. It's not true because Charlie is a genius philosopher; nor is it true scientifically. Instead, it seems like Charlie just got lucky with much of what he said. This is very interesting, since philosophers today have not really solved this problem of epistemic luck.

Let's just give a quick example handed down to us by the philosopher who highlighted this phenomena in the 1960s, Edmund Gettier. Imagine you're at home, and your friend comes over worrying that his watch is broken. He asks you the time, and you look at the clock, reporting that it is 4:10pm. He checks his watch too, and confirms your reading. Now it turns out that in this particular case, the friend's watch isn't in fact broken, and it's accurately reporting the time, 4:10pm. However, the clock you checked is broken, and just happened to have stop working with the hands pointing to 4:10pm! In this case, we verified that the friend's watch was working based on faulty reasoning—consulting a broken device—but luckily it turned out to be true! This scenario is quite disturbing, since it makes us wonder how we can ever be sure that any of our reasoning is not faulty; we have no way to know if we are consulting a broken device or not when we are examining anything in the universe, and that anything we know seems true could just be dumb luck.

This throws a ratchet into what we think philosophy might be. Ideally, we want philosophy to be the result of careful reasoning using true premises, and conclusions actually following from premises—but we can never be sure we have reasoned carefully enough or that our premises are true! Perhaps it's the case that we never can verify anything we know about the world, but rather continuous falsify what others claim to have discovered. This point was raised by Aristotle himself in response to Plato's theory of forms, which was a highly abstract explanation of the fundamental nature of the universe. Aristotle notes something along the lines of "we can never determine what something is, only what it is not."

This statement exactly nails down why *It's Always Sunny* is in fact philosophical. Everything the Gang does is the exact opposite of the way the world is. Everything the Gang believes is the exact opposite of everything that's true! And the way the Gang acts is the exact opposite of everything we should do. *It's Always Sunny* presents the antithesis to reality . . . and that is *absolutely* philosophical.

I

Good

1
The Ancient Art of Being an Asshole

GREG LITTMANN

What a bunch of assholes! The Gang dig up graves, exploit the welfare system, run sweatshops, shoot people, kidnap people, poison their flip cup rivals, impersonate police to steal money, and attempt murder and cannibalism, among other adventures in selfishness and depravity.

Members of the Gang often notice their friends' bastardry, and often point it out, so routinely so that in the Gang's homebrewed game "CharDee MacDennis", the official answer to the question "Dennis is asshole. Why Charlie hate?" is "Because Dennis is a bastard man." But members of the Gang are blind to their own shitty behavior.

Mac sees himself as the bar "sheriff," keeping order with his bad-assery. Frank sees himself as a cunning winner in a dog-eat-dog competitive environment. "This is America: you're either a duper or a dupee," he explains to Mac in "Gun Fever Too: Still Hot." Dennis is so arrogant that when he enters a sensory deprivation tank in "Charlie Rules the World", he has a mystical experience in which he meets himself and learns that he is God. Charlie and Dee are not always brimming with self-esteem like Mac, Dennis, and Frank; but it is not their own nasty behavior that bothers them: rather, it's the way that the world treats them. Given a chance to escape their lowly positions in life—as Charlie does as a king in an online game in "Charlie Rules the World" and Dee does as a

3

comedian in "The Gang Broke Dee"—they become as arrogant as Dennis. Abandoning the Gang after being offered Hollywood fame, Dee sneers, "You made me? I made you! Screw you guys, all right?"

One of the things that makes the Gang's values so philosophically interesting is how closely they resemble the values we find in the earliest western literature, the heroic epics the *Iliad* and *Odyssey* by the Greek poet Homer. Set around the thirteenth century B.C.E., the *Iliad* tells the story of a war between a confederation of Greek kings and the city of Troy, while the *Odyssey* tells the story of King Odysseus's long journey home after the war. The Gang are held up to us as ridiculous people, but Homer's warriors, who are not so different, are presented as examples of life lived *excellently*. How can it be that ancient *heroes* so closely resemble those evil fuckers from Paddy's pub? In fact, Homeric values are not only a part of the Gang's value system, but of the value system of much of the modern world. The earliest western moral philosophy was a response to a society with values that were still largely Homeric. Guys like Socrates, Plato, and Aristotle could see that Homeric values are for assholes and wanted to find a better way for humans to behave. We still need philosophy to help us turn away from the ancient assholishness in modern form so clearly demonstrated by the Gang at Paddy's Pub and so prevalent in our society. Alright, so what *are* the Gang's values? What do the Gang think is important in life?

The Gang Makes Lethal Weapon 6

The most obvious measure of success in life for the Gang is money. Many episodes revolve around their latest get-rich-quick scheme. In "The Gang Solves the Gas Crisis", they try to make cash by selling gas door-to-door, in "Mac and Dennis Buy a Time Share," the pair try to manipulate the property market, and in "Paddy's Pub: Home of the Original Kitten Mittens" the Gang tries to copyright socks for cats. Even the uncomfortable prospect of Paddy's becoming a gay bar in

"The Gang Gets Racist" is tolerable given the profits at stake. When Frank loses his fortune in "The Great Recession", he decides that life is no longer worth living and tries to hang himself.

Homeric heroes agree that being rich is an important goal in life. As Odysseus's son Telemachus says in the *Odyssey*, "It is no bad thing to be a king—to see one's house enriched and one's authority enhanced." When Telemachus visits the home of Menelaus, wealthy king of Sparta, he raves about the bling to his friend Peisistratus—"The whole place gleams with bronze and gold, amber and silver and ivory. What an amazing quantity of treasures! The court of Zeus on Olympus must be like this inside." Like the Gang, many of the heroes' adventures focus on making money, though the Greeks use the much bloodier means of sacking foreign cities and taking their stuff.

But money isn't all there is to life. The Gang want attention too! It is easy to see them as self-centered, but in fact, a lot of their focus is directed towards others, because they care so much about what other people think of them. It is true, they don't *always* care about appearances in every situation in which most people would care: In "A Very Sunny Christmas" Frank is happy to emerge naked from a couch into a room full of people for the sake of getting cool, while in "The Gang Desperately Tries to Win an Award," the Gang enthusiastically spits on their patrons to drive them from the pub. More often, though, their need for positive attention is desperate. Whether trying out for the Philadelphia Eagles, making their own news videos and lethal weapon movies, fighting to get a bar award, or starring in Charlie's musical, *Nightman Cometh*, the Gang seize any exposure they can get. Charlie encapsulates their attitude in "The Gang Makes Lethal Weapon 6," observing, "Why make anything, you know? For the money, for the glory, for the fame!"

Dee, who is always looking for her break into show-business, has produced several talent contests in the hopes that she will eventually win one. In "The Gang Saves the Day" she fantasizes a perfect life for herself, in which she is a famous Hollywood actor being praised on a television talk show. In "America's Next Top Paddy's Billboard Model Contest," her humiliation at having her private diary published on the internet turns to joy when Charlie informs her that she's had eighty thousand hits. Likewise, on "Mac Day," when the Gang has to do whatever Mac wants, what he wants most is attention. They are forced to do things like listen as he reads from the Bible and gives them a long lecture on the sin of homosexuality (while sporting an erection). As for Frank, he's so arrogant that he'll only fund *Lethal Weapon 5* and *6* if they allow him to star.

Likewise for the Greek heroes, glory is central to their lives—public glory is what being a hero is all about! When Achilles's father, King Peleus, sends him off to war, he instructs him "Now always be the best, my boy, the bravest, and hold your head up high above the others." In fact, as a youth Achilles was offered a choice between a short but glorious life and a long and comfortable life without glory; he chose glory without hesitation. For the Greeks, worthiness for fame is measured in lethality and material success. Odysseus boasts, "We are proud to belong to the forces of Agamemnon, Atreus's son, who by sacking the great city of Troy and destroying all its armies has made himself the most famous man in the world today." Fighting for glory is fiercely competitive and people are not shy about making comparisons. When the Trojan champion Hector is killed by Achilles, Hector's mother and father openly complain in front of Hector's brothers that they have not only lost a son, they've lost the *best one*. Old Nestor criticizes Achilles for caring only about his reputation instead of his comrades. He's got a point—Achilles once expresses his wish that everyone in both armies should die in the war except for him and his best friend Patroklos, so that there would be more glory for them.

Many Greek heroes even aspire, like Dennis, to godhood. After all, as Dennis points out after his mystical experience, "the only thing bigger than a king is a god." Dennis is more arrogant than the Greeks though, because he thinks himself to be fully God, like Jesus and Jim Jones, while the greatest Greek heroes made do with being only partly divine. Achilles and Heracles, for instance, were half gods, Achilles being the son of the nymph Thetis and Heracles the son of Zeus, while Odysseus is a more modest eighth God, as the great-grandson of the god Hermes. (The Mesopotamian hero Gilgamesh makes the strange claim of being two-thirds god, suggesting some sort of weird gangbang involving two bisexual gods and a mortal whom nobody is ever going to believe).

Project Badass

The Gang compete for glory in many ways, but perhaps the most traditional is the need to be thought a badass. Mac wants a reputation as a badass so much that he directs a series of "Project Badass" videos in which he pretends to perform dangerous stunts, like jumping off the Strawberry Mansion Bridge and riding a bicycle over a ramp while wearing pyrotechnics. Mac frequently boasts about his "blackbelt" karate skills and casually throws punches at the air. When he lands the role of the Nightman in Charlie's musical, *The Nightman Cometh*, he reworks the character to his own tastes—"The Nightman's badass, dude! He has the eyes of a cat and does karate across the stage!" Mac even dresses to make the point, tattooing a dragon and an eagle on his arms and wearing sleeveless shirts that show off his biceps. The shirts are often printed with an image conveying danger or machismo, like skulls and cobras, or even the challenge "What are you looking at, dicknose?" Fantasizing during a convenience store robbery in "The Gang Saves the Day," Mac beats up an army of ninja with his superhuman abilities. Allowed to build a fantasy life for himself in an online game in "Charlie Rules the World," he wants to live as a huge thug who slaps around everyone else in the game. "I've always wanted to be six foot ten" he confides.

Mac's not the only one with tough-guy fantasies. Dennis joins Mac as a manhunter in "Mac and Dennis: Manhunters" and Charlie joins him as a vigilante in "Gun Fever Too: Still

Hot." In the same episode, Frank revels in playing the hero on television after scaring away some muggers with his gun. Even Dee is as impressed as the rest of the gang in "The Gang Gets Racist" when she thinks that her new boyfriend started and won a bar fight.

For the Greeks, it's impossible to be a hero if you aren't a bad-ass, and the bigger a bad-ass you are, the greater a hero you are. One man is simply called "better" than another if he's better at fighting. A really first-rate hero like Achilles or Odysseus will take on and vanquish hordes of enemy soldiers, like Mac defeating his hordes of ninja. Even Mac's fantasy of being six foot ten leaves him dwarfed by the Greek hero Ajax, who is at least nine feet tall. Not putting up a fight is considered a terrible shame. In the *Iliad*, Greek leaders routinely appeal to the sense of glory and shame of their troops when urging them to fight, asking them to consider what their families and other people will say about them. The great Greek warrior Diomedes says that he'd rather have the earth open up and swallow him than for an enemy to go around saying that he was too scared to fight them. It's a sentiment that warriors express throughout the *Iliad*. Achilles and Diomedes and the rest would surely join the Gang in laughing at Mac for pooping himself when a street fight breaks out in "Mac Day."

Just as Mac frequently wears shirts with violent or macho images, so the Greek heroes decorated their armor to make a statement about who they were. Odysseus relates the time he met the ghost of Heracles—"Terrible was the golden belt he wore as a baldric over his breast, depicting miraculous scenes—bears, wild boars and glaring lions, conflict and battle, bloodshed and the massacre of men." There's no point being bad-ass if people don't realize it!

Dennis Reynolds: An Erotic Life

Dennis's favorite form of glory is the glory he gets from banging women. He measures his success in life by the number he's slept with. He even makes secret video recordings of his adventures and spends most of the running time showing off to the camera. Ideally, he would like to go public with his achievements by publishing his memoirs, "Dennis Reynolds: An Erotic Life." Other members of the Gang have a similar attitude to sexual glory. In "America's Next Top Paddy's Billboard Model Contest," Frank sets up a billboard to advertise Paddy's Pub, featuring himself framed by two enormous pairs of breasts. In "Charlie Got Molested," Mac's vanity is offended when he believes that Charlie was molested as a child, because he himself apparently wasn't attractive enough to get molested. He complains, "If the McPoyles got blown and Charlie got blown, why didn't I get blown?"

The Greek heroes, too, were admired for their sexual prowess. When Odysseus gets lost on his way back from the Trojan War, he spends ten years slowly banging his way around the Mediterranean. To be fair, what he really wants is to get home to his wife, but the way that the gorgeous ladies refuse to leave him alone serves to demonstrate what an astonishing stud he is. Like Dennis, the Greek heroes don't regard a woman's consent as essential to scoring glory by having sex with her. Women are routinely given away to heroes as war trophies. In fact, the *Iliad* centers on an argument about who gets the honor of being awarded the priestess Briseis as a slave. The most powerful Greek king, Agamemnon, takes her away from Achilles, whose honor is so hurt that he refuses to fight anymore. Achilles makes it clear that he has no particular attachment to Briseis herself. Rather, like Mac being angry at not being blown at school along with the McPoyles, it's the insult to his worthiness that Achilles can't bear.

Winners Always Win

Obsessions with machismo and sexual conquest are only the tip of the Gang's need to compete. When Molly's Pub won't play them at the Flipadelphia Flip Cup championships, the gang invades Molly's and starts abusing the patrons. In "CharDee MacDennis", a game of the Gang's own devising, contestants must, among other things, hold their hand on a dartboard without flinching or showing pain while their opponents throw darts, and endure hours of emotional abuse, in Dee's case to the point that she once cried for a month and attempted suicide. Why didn't she just give up? The game is too important! As she explains when the Gang gets hooked on an online computer game in "Charlie Rules the World," "It's like when I'm doing good in the game, I'm doing good in life." Charlie goes further: "I think we can all agree that this game is the most important thing that has ever happened to us."

Competition is not always so formal. When Mac and Dennis get a medical checkup in "Frank's Pretty Woman," Mac cares less about his own diabetes than he does about the fact that he's healthier than Dennis. When Dee learns in "The Aluminum Monster vs. Fatty McGoo" that her old childhood friend "Fatty McGoo" has become a successful clothes designer, she has to plot to ruin her.

Likewise, the Greek heroes saw no need to limit their competition to the battlefield. Sports were no less popular in the Bronze Age than they are today and the Greek heroes doubled as sports stars. The warriors of the *Iliad* turn the funeral of their friend Patroklos into a sporting event in which they can show off, just as Mac makes his cousin Country Mac's funeral all about himself. Like an ancient sportscast, the epic fills us in on stories such as how Diomedes outdrove Antilochus in the chariot race, and how Ajax and Odysseus wrestled each other to a standstill. Just as the Gang and other modern sports fans invest themselves in the teams they support, so ancient audiences of the *Iliad* would be keeping track of the victories of their ancestors, rooting for them and basking in their glory. The offense the Gang takes at not winning a pub award in "The Gang Tries Desperately to Win an Award" pales in comparison to the importance the Greeks place on prizes. The old hero Nestor relates how in his youth, he fought in a war over a disputed horse racing trophy, while Ajax is so offended at not being awarded the armor of Achilles after Achilles's death that he plots to kill the surviving Greek heroes, his former friends and allies. Of course, the Gang know all about the need for revenge!

The Gang's Revenge

When the Gang believe that they've been wronged, they must seek vengeance. For example, in "Charlie Has Cancer," Dee will only agree to help Mac if Mac lets her punch him in the face, as payback for Mac accidentally punching her in the face. When Mac learns that Charlie has been smashing his "Project Badass" tapes in "Mac's Banging the Waitress," Mac . . . well, he decides to bang the Waitress. Likewise, when Charlie and Dennis are shushed in a bar in "The ANTI-social Network," they try to track the shusher down to beat him up, and when that fails, go to the police and tell them that the shusher raped them. For Frank, revenge is an art. When he gets pissed off with Dee and Dennis for making fun of his creeping senility in "Charlie's Mom Has Cancer," he gets his own back by tricking them into digging up their mother's corpse. On other occasions, the Gang all seek revenge together, as in "The High School Reunion, Part 2: The Gang's Revenge", in which they try to get their own back, by means violent, sexual, and musical, on all those who had wronged them at school. As Frank explains "Look, if life pushes you down, you got to push back. If you're dealt a bunch of lemons, you got to take those lemons and stuff them down somebody's throat until they see yellow. And if some punk-ass kid humiliates you, you got to do the only thing that's left to do."

The Greek heroes likewise believed that honor demands revenge. Achilles sacrifices his life to avenge the death of his friend Patroklos, who was impaled on a spear in battle by the Trojan hero Hector. Achilles knows that he's fated to die soon after Hector does, but that doesn't stop him from ramming his own spear through Hector's throat and dragging his dead enemy's corpse around behind his chariot for three days (an act of corpse desecration that makes Frank flushing Country Mac down the toilet look respectful).

When Odysseus finally makes it back to his kingdom of Ithaca after twenty years away, his first act is to brutally slay all the men who have tried to court his wife while he's been gone. He hacks down the fleeing suitors until he "stood among the corpses of the dead, spattered with blood and gore, like a lion when he comes from feeding on some farmer's bullock, with the blood dripping from his breast and jaws on either side, a fearsome spectacle." Then for good measure, he rounds up all the palace maids who had fraternized with the young men and hangs them in a row, then tracks down a goatherd he suspects of collaboration and has his men cut off the poor bastard's ears, nose, dick, hands, and feet. As it happens, the queen has stayed true to her absent husband, despite the passage of two decades without a word from him, but it would be fascinating to know what he would have done to her if she hadn't been! Even Frank's trick of getting Dennis and Dee to dig up their own dead mother is small potatoes to the Greeks. When Agamemnon's father Atreus finds out that his wife is having an affair with his brother Thyestes, Atreus kills and cooks up Thyestes sons, and then tricks Thyestes into eating them for dinner.

Let's Get Dirty

When the Gang compete, all they care about is winning, not how dirty they have to play to win. Cheating successfully just makes them proud of their cleverness. As revealed in "A Very Sunny Christmas," Frank only got rich in the first place by stealing from his ex-partner. Likewise, though Mac sees himself as "sheriff" of Paddy's, we see in "The Gang Gets Whacked" that he idolizes mafiosi and would do anything to join the mob. In "Dennis and Dee Go on Welfare" the pair exploit the welfare system, while Charlie breaks a rich girl's heart in "Charlie and Dee Find Love" just to make the waitress jealous. In fact, one of the most common premises for episodes is that the Gang is running a new scam, as in "Charlie Gets Crippled," "The Gang Exploit a Miracle," and "The Gang Runs for Office." Dennis sums up their attitude in "The Gang Dances Their Asses Off"—"Look, there's no point in taking any chances. Let's get dirty."

Likewise, the Greek heroes care about winning itself, not how it is achieved. Like the Gang, they believe that successfully cheating an enemy only demonstrates how clever you are. Odysseus boasts: "I am . . . known to all for my deceptive skills—my fame extends all the way to heaven." The Trojan War itself only comes to an end, after ten long years, when Odysseus comes up with the idea of getting past the city walls of Troy by building a gigantic wooden horse in which the Greek soldiers could hide, tricking the Trojans into taking it into their city as a gift from the gods. Later, Odysseus defeats the man-eating Cyclops Polyphemos by fooling him into getting drunk, stabbing him in his single eye while he's asleep, and escaping by hiding under a ram. In "CharDee MacDennis," the Gang permits cheating, providing that the cheater's not caught. Odysseus takes the same attitude to sports. He wins a footrace at the funeral games of Patroklos by praying to the goddess Athena to fix the race for him. "Ajax slipped at a dead run—Athena tripped him up—right where the dung lay slick from bellowing cattle . . . Dung stuffed his mouth, his nostrils dripped muck as shining long-enduring Odysseus flashed past him." Why was it necessary for the goddess to give Ajax a face full of poop along with his pratfall? My guess is that Homer would answer as Frank does in "Who Pooped the Bed?" when asked why he's been pooping the bed he shares with Charlie: "Because poop is funny!"

Dee, We Don't Care about You

The Gang are assholes even to one another. To be fair, on rare occasions, they will display small signs of sympathy for their friends. In "Charlie Kelly: King of the Rats," when the Gang sees that Charlie is unusually depressed, they decide to make him feel good for a day "in the simplest, easiest way" by arranging a spa day and a surprise birthday party (though it turns out that Frank is tricking them into throwing a "surprise party" for *him*). More typical, though, is their reaction to Dee's depression in "The Gang Broke Dee," in which they try to change Dee's irritating behavior by raising her hopes and then shattering them again, fooling her into thinking that she has become a successful comedian, only to suddenly and publicly reveal that it has all been a hoax. In "Who Got Dee Pregnant?" Mac makes the rest of the guys' feelings for Dee explicit, telling her, "Dee, we don't care about you or your body or your baby . . . or that baby bird that you're probably carrying inside of you."

Other members of the Gang don't fare much better. When Frank tries to hang himself in "The Great Recession," nobody cares except for Charlie, who objects on a practical point—Frank's neck is too fat for hanging to work. Likewise, when the gang believes that Charlie has become a genius in "Flowers for Charlie," they not only aren't happy for him, but plot to force him back into his old, mundane life, so that he can do the lowly "Charlie work" for them. Frank explains: "Charlie is our foundation. Where does a foundation belong? On the bottom. We gotta go grab Charlie and drag him back down into the sewer where he belongs!" In fact, a number of episodes are studies in mutual betrayal, as alliances form and dissolve between members of the Gang. When the bar is held up in "The Gang Gets Held Hostage," first the three guys try to sacrifice Dee to save themselves, then Dennis sells Mac and Dennis out, plotting with Dee to sacrifice them, then Dee sells Dennis out in a plot with Charlie, while all the while Mac tries to ally with Frank to sacrifice everyone else.

It's in their loyalty to their friends that the Greek heroes show their greatest difference from the Gang. For warriors of the Bronze Age, as for soldiers today, survival depended on being able to rely on the people around you in battle, and the powerful bonds of loyalty forged between warriors provide the closest relationships Homer shows us. Like Frank and Charlie sharing an apartment, Achilles and his best buddy, Patroklos, share a tent on the field before Troy. When Frank thinks that Charlie is dead in "Mac and Charlie Die," he's upset enough to build a fake Charlie to cry on and hump, but when Patroklos is killed by Hector, Achilles is willing to sacrifice his own life for payback. In the *Odyssey*, Odysseus's son Telemachus visits his father's old military buddies from the Trojan War, looking for help finding his dad, who didn't arrive home. Nestor, king of Pylos, and Menelaus, king of Sparta, greet the son of their old friend like a friend himself, and are willing to do anything they can to aid him. In a world without police officers and frequently without laws, informal bonds like these are essential for any sort of safety. If Odysseus's friends had not stood up for him, there would have been nobody else to turn to. Even when Odysseus does make it home, reclaiming his kingdom requires gathering his friends together on the battlefield to enforce his legitimate claim to the throne.

Wow, You're a Horrible Father!

The Gang care no more for members of their family than they do for their friends. Even when Frank believed that Dee and Dennis are his natural children, he still didn't care about them. As we find out in "A Very Sunny Christmas," Christmas for Dee and Dennis as children consisted in seeing Frank give the presents they most wanted to *himself*, while they got nothing. "Merry Christmas, bitches!" he cries on a video of Christmas '86, as the kids open their empty boxes. No wonder the only way Frank can get anyone to visit him in hospital is to fake his own death. As noted above, Dennis and Dee care nothing for each other, though they are brother and sister, and will sell each other out as quickly as they will sell out anyone else. Likewise, when Charlie is told that he has a son in "Charlie Wants an Abortion," he doesn't want to know him and cares nothing about him, seeing him only as a tool to win over the waitress. When he learns that Tommy is not really his son, he feels only relief. Nor do Mac and Charlie care much about their mothers. Charlie notes in "Charlie's Mom has Cancer," "We don't talk and it's good that way."

For the Greek heroes, looking after family is an essential part of life lived well. In a world with little law and order and no social services, anyone without a family to protect and support them is in trouble, and family bonds of loyalty are strong. The Trojan War would not have been fought in the first place if the great king Agamemnon had not agreed to help avenge his brother Menelaus after Menelaus's wife Helen ran off with a Trojan prince. Telemachus undertakes a perilous journey across Greece to gain help in his quest to save Odysseus. Odysseus, in turn, is driven to take back his kingdom so that he can pass it on to his son. Odysseus feels no less loyalty to his mother and father. He tells King Alcinous, "a man's fatherland and his parents are what he holds sweetest, even though he has settled far away from his people in some rich home." On the other hand, according to the goddess Athena, women in the Bronze Age were less sentimental. Athena tells Telemachus, "You know what a woman's disposition is. She likes to bring riches to the house of the man who is marrying her, but never remembers or asks about the dead husband she once loved or the children she bore him."

The Gang Give Back

The gang often becomes self-righteous over social issues to flatter their egos. In "Gun Fever Too: Still Hot" they try to solve the gun problem, in "The Gang Wrestles for the Troops," they try to help veterans, and in "Charlie Goes America All Over Everybody's Ass," Charlie fights public smoking. But they don't really care about their community or about strangers any more than they care about one another. Nothing demonstrates this more clearly than the way they treat kids. In "Underage Drinking: A National Concern," they let children drink at Paddy's, in "Dee Reynolds: Shaping America's Youth" they show school students a porn movie, and in "The Gang Gives Back" they teach underprivileged kids how to cheat at sports by injuring their opponents.

The attitude of the Greek heroes is not that different. Unlike the Gang, they do often care about their immediate community. Most of the heroes are kings who protect the well-being of those they reign over, slaying monsters and dispensing justice as necessary. Whereas Mac cares so little about his duty as a voter that his positions on abortion and the environment are determined by his chances of scoring with women, Odysseus is praised as a gentle and compassionate king, a "loving father" to the people of Ithaca who ruled with "never an injustice to a single person in the land." On the other hand, when the heroes deal with people outside of their own communities, their sympathies vanish. To the Greek heroes, foreign cities are a source of glory and treasure. Their armies are to be defeated and their homes sacked. Sometimes, as in the case of Troy, they kill all the men and carry the women and children off into slavery, seeing them as just part of the treasure to be won. Having no relationship with these people, the Greek heroes care nothing about them.

We're Gonna Go America All Over Their Asses!

So much for comparing the Gang's values to Homeric values. What does any of it have to do with our *own* lives? Obviously, like the Gang and Bronze Age Greeks, modern Westerners still often spend their lives chasing money and status, or striving to be the center of attention. But the really interesting thing about comparing common modern values with those of the gang and the Homeric Greeks is the degree to which the differences lie in the *scope* of our moral concerns.

What shocks us about both the behavior of the Gang and the behavior of Greek heroes is their selfishness and their callousness toward others. Members of the Gang care only for themselves, to the point that they don't mind if even their closest friends and family are suicidal. The Greek heroes care for their friends and family, and defend their communities from outside threats, but care nothing for people they have no relationship with, to the point that plundering a foreign city and killing the inhabitants is admired as badass.

Most modern westerners have an even wider scope of moral concern. Unlike the Gang but like the Greeks, we think that people should care about their friends and family, treating them with kindness and loyalty. Unlike both the Gang and the Greeks, we generally feel some moral responsibilities even to outsiders. The public would not tolerate vigilantes targeting the homeless, as Mac and Dee do in "Bums: Making a Mess All Over the City." Nor could a modern western power plunder a foreign city and lead its inhabitants off into slavery as the Greek heroes would.

Yet we still base our degree of concern for people on the degree of our relationship with them, often treating people we have least relationship with in the way that the Greeks treat outsiders and the gang treats everybody. Most of all, we care about our friends and family. If we care about our communities at all, we care much less about our fellow citizens than we do about our personal circle. Not many of us would let a family member go homeless or tolerate a friend being raped, but we tolerate homelessness on our streets and rape in our prisons.

Citizens of foreign nations count least of all. Just as wealthy Frank is content to let his poor friend Charlie rely on homemade vitamin "energy balls" to avoid starvation, and the Greek heroes are content to hoard their treasure rather than sharing with their hungry peasants, we are largely content to stand by as people in other countries starve, seeing their problems as nothing to do with us. Just as the Gang are happy to profit from running a sweatshop in "The Aluminum Monster vs. Fatty McGoo," and the Greek heroes were happy to profit from the forced labor of their slaves, we are generally happy to be supplied with goods produced by exploited workers—provided that they come from overseas. Just as the Gang and the Greek heroes revel in being arrogant on the personal level, we revel in our arrogance on the national level. We love to see our country glorified and to see our nation outperform other nations and to triumph over them. Just as the gang sees glory in someone starting and winning a bar fight, and the Greeks see glory in military conquest, we often show more enthusiasm for rooting for our side in warfare and celebrating military victory than we do for making sure that our wars are just, or worrying about the suffering inflicted on our troops, enemy soldiers, and civilian populations.

The big difference between ourselves and the Gang is not that we care and they don't, but that they care only for themselves. Likewise, our big difference from the Greek heroes is that they care only about those they have relationships with, while we often show at least some concern for strangers. Where our morals fail, though, they fail in the same basic way as the morals of the Gang and of the heroes—when people are far enough removed from us, we just stop caring. What we need, and what philosophy can offer us, are some universal moral principles to help us move beyond being assholes and do right by *everyone*. Early Greek moral philosophers sniffed out the asshole lying at the center of the butt of conventional morality, but 2,500 years later, that asshole still stinks. Bleaching your asshole, as Artemis does, is not enough. You must pick up the soap of universal morality and get your asshole clean.

2
No Restrictions, Baby!

JASON IULIANO

Pleasure. The Gang desires this one thing. It motivates their every action. From shifting alliances to disregarding responsibilities to manipulating others, the gang's every move is directed towards maximizing pleasure.

This pursuit of pleasure is on full display when Mac enters the bar fifty pounds heavier at the start of Season Seven ("Frank's Pretty Woman"). While gorging on a trash bag full of chimichangas and injecting insulin into his stomach, Mac discusses his "No restrictions" philosophy with Dennis. At one point, Mac asks Dennis, "What do you want more than anything else in the entire world?" When Dennis says he'd like to smoke crack, the two of them shout, "Let's do it! No restrictions, Baby!"

At their core, Mac, Dennis, Charlie, Dee, and Frank are hedonists. They take whatever actions they think will cause them the greatest immediate pleasure and even feel morally justified in prioritizing pleasure above all else. The Gang's philosophy of life boils down to a pretty straightforward principle: maximize pleasure and minimize pain. This ethical system sounds pretty inviting, doesn't it? Not only are you permitted to do whatever gives you the most pleasure, you are morally required to do so.

Feel like skipping work tomorrow to drink beer and eat milk steak? Go for it! In love with the newest Lamborghini

Countach? Just take out a loan and drive that beauty off the lot tonight! Want to break into an Asian family's home to steal a vase? You'd be morally blameworthy for not doing it! Hell, have a desire to smoke crack? No restrictions, Baby!

It's All Greek

Are Dennis, Mac, Charlie, Dee, and Frank terrible people? No! Alright, well maybe. But it might surprise you to know that they're extremely ethical. They strictly follow the moral tenets of egoistic hedonism. If you've ever wondered how the Gang can sleep soundly at night given all the "immoral" things they do, this is the answer. The Gang isn't acting immorally, so they have no reason to feel guilty. All of their seemingly evil actions are explainable and even praiseworthy when viewed from the perspective of egoistic hedonism.

The Gang's pathological pursuit of pleasure finds its roots in Ancient Greece. Although there are several varieties of hedonism, the gang's specific version (egoistic hedonism) got its start way back in Athens around 400 B.C. Back then, a disciple of Socrates named Aristippus posed the question: What's the purpose of human life?

This seems like a question that should have an answer. After all, every action we take is oriented towards some end. The purpose of drinking fight milk is to become a bigger, stronger bodyguard ("Frank's Back in Business"). The purpose of putting kitten mittens on your cats is to stop their unnaturally loud stomping ("Paddy's Pub: Home of the Original Kitten Mittens"). Given that all of our actions have some goal, it only seems natural that human life itself should be oriented towards some end. So, what is that end?

Aristippus concluded that the goal of human life is to experience happiness and that our desire to experience happiness motivates our actions. This, however, raised yet another question: What exactly is happiness? Is it, perhaps, the pursuit of virtuous activities? That's what Aristotle maintained. In his view, happiness is achieved by cultivating virtues of the soul—wisdom, generosity, temperance, honesty, courage, and the like. Aristippus, however, fervently disagreed with this conception. Happiness, he believed, is something much more tangible. Happiness is pleasure.

Like all true hedonists, Aristippus argued that there is a direct connection between happiness and pleasure. In his view, pleasure is the highest human value and the only one that can make us truly happy. And so, pleasure is the only thing that is intrinsically good. All other goods are merely instrumental. They are good only insofar as they help us attain pleasure. Therefore, to maximize happiness, we should pursue actions that provide the most net pleasure after pain is subtracted. So far, this is pretty standard for hedonists of all stripes.

However, where Aristippus and his followers (the Cyrenaics) differed is in his prioritization of present, personal, bodily pleasures. There are three distinctions to be drawn here. First, Aristippus is focused on pleasures in the present. From his perspective, everyone should live for the moment and discount future consequences. You may notice an element of *carpe diem* here that intensely captures the Gang's complete and utter lack of foresight (or more charitably their desire to live every day to the fullest, future consequences be damned).

Second, whereas other hedonists placed greater weight on mental pleasures, Aristippus and the Cyrenaics focused on the bodily sort. They did so because they viewed bodily pleasures as more intense and trustworthy. Sex, drugs, and rock'n'roll could very well be the Aristippian mantra. It is not selfish to indulge in bodily pleasures, rather it's the path to the good life. This is right up the Gang's alley. After all, when's the last time any of them were concerned with mental pleasures? I mean, Charlie can't even read!

Now, before you say I'm wrong and point to Dennis's intellectual prowess, you better think again, Jabroni. Admittedly, Dennis is proud of his University of Pennsylvania degree and is always willing to brag about his minor in psychology ("Charlie Got Molested"). However, Dennis is all about appearances. He doesn't actually care for the life of the mind. He just wants people to perceive him as smart. Dennis gets pleasure from feeling superior to others and having people recognize him as such. Therefore, what at first seems like a mental pleasure is actually nothing more than a base bodily pleasure. Dennis is a thoroughgoing Aristippian hedonist.

A third unique feature of Aristippus' theory is that he ascribes value only to his own personal pleasure. His ethical theory allowed him to completely disregard the good or bad effects of his actions on others. All that mattered was his own pleasure. The gang members strictly adhere to this principle. Unwavering pursuit of their own happiness allows them to disregard everyone else—even each other—without the slightest hint of guilt.

These three features are core components of Aristippus's hedonism. They are also central to how Dennis, Mac, Charlie, Dee, and Frank live their lives.

Poor Rickety Cricket

Like true egoistic hedonists, the Gang has no concern for anyone else's wellbeing. They're focused solely on their own individual pleasure, and nowhere is this more evident than in their interactions with Rickety Cricket. Their abuse of Cricket goes all the way back to high school when Dee told Cricket that she would kiss him if he ate a horse turd. After Cricket ate the turd, Dee reneged because "his breath smelled like shit" ("The Gang Exploits a Miracle"). Dee, however, hasn't been the only one to humiliate Cricket for her own pleasure. For years, Mac and Dennis have been taking pictures of themselves teabagging Cricket. The two have done this so frequently, that Dennis claims to have filled an entire shoebox with pictures of the teabaggings ("Mac and Dennis: Manhunters").

The Gang sees nothing wrong in using other people as mere devices to enhance their own pleasure. They can't even understand why Cricket could possibly be upset by how he's treated. When Cricket shows up to the Gang's Thanksgiving dinner in order to squash his beefs, Mac is confused and asks Cricket, "What the hell are you doing here? We don't have beef with you." Cricket is stunned by Mac's comment and shows his frustration, saying, "You don't have beef with me? I was a priest before I got involved with you guys. Unbelievable." ("The Gang Squashes Their Beefs").

Indeed, before Cricket got involved with the Gang, he was living a rather good life as a priest. However, by the time the Gang had their way with him, Cricket's life had been ruined. He had become homeless, had his legs broken by the mob ("The Gang Gets Whacked [Part 2]"), been hunted like an animal by Mac and Dennis ("Mac and Dennis: Manhunters"), and had his throat slashed with a trashcan by Frank ("The Gang Wrestles for the Troops"). The Gang had completely destroyed Cricket's life, but they felt no moral misgivings about doing so. Cricket was nothing more than an object to be used and abused for the gang's enjoyment.

This lack of concern for the welfare of anyone else is a core feature of egoistic hedonism. Like the gang, Aristippus viewed others as mere instruments to aid in his pursuit of pleasure.

The Gang Pursues Pleasure . . . and Fails

You could pick any episode at random to illustrate the Gang's hedonistic proclivities. However, let's look at a few that best capture the Gang's self-destructive drive for immediate gratification. Hopefully you'll agree that this core aspect of Aristippus's philosophy is actually undermining the gang's ability to find happiness.

Let's start with "The Gang Buys a Boat." Here, Mac, Dennis, and Charlie take the $2,500 they earned from dicktowel.com to go boat shopping. When the salesman offers a boat that clearly fails to meet their requirements (Mac's "need for speed" and Dennis's desire to host "P. Diddy-style parties"), they rush to purchase it anyway. The three of them are so blinded by their quest for pleasure that they lack any ability to delay gratification by turning down the boat and making better use of the money at a future time.

Dennis acknowledges as much when he says, "We've had our hearts set on this boat thing for days now which in our world is a level of focus which I personally have never experienced." Dennis, Mac, and Charlie are so pleasure-driven that they don't pause to consider how hard it will be to turn the dilapidated vessel into their dream yacht (or, in Charlie's case, dream shrimping boat). Instead, they simply live in the moment. The guys want a boat, and damn it they are going to buy a boat.

Irrational purchases aren't the only evidence of the Gang's obsession with immediate gratification. We also observe it in their unwillingness to work hard to improve their future. Instead of grinding it out and turning the bar into a successful business, the Gang tries to take the easy way out by concocting countless get-rich-quick schemes.

The examples are legion and have made for some of the most memorable episodes in the series. For instance, in "The Gang Exploits a Miracle," Mac finds a water stain in the office that looks like the Virgin Mary, and the gang tries to make a quick buck off of this coincidence by charging admission to view it. Another scheme is put into action when the city's trash men go on strike. This time, the Gang tries to take advantage of the situation by collecting garbage from rich Philadelphians ("The Gang Recycles Their Trash"). Likewise, in "The Gang Solves the Gas Crisis," Mac, Dennis, and Charlie try to exploit high gas prices by traveling around in Frank's rape van, attempting to sell gasoline door-to-door.

In yet another episode, Dennis and Dee quit their jobs at the pub to pursue their dream professions ("Dennis and Dee Go on Welfare"). However, when they realize that they can make more from unemployment benefits and that achieving their dream jobs takes hard work, the two of them decide it's easier just to exploit the system for their own personal gain. Although Mac momentarily derails their plan when he tells them that unemployment eventually runs out, it doesn't deter Dennis and Dee for long. They quickly devise a plan to start smoking crack cocaine in order to scam the welfare system.

Each of these episodes provides insight into the Gang's motivations, but perhaps the most revealing get-rich-quick scheme is when Dennis runs for the position of local comptroller in order to solicit bribes ("The Gang Runs for Office"). The Gang's plan is not inspired by any sort of altruistic concern. Instead, they are purely interested in their own well-being and pleasure. This is apparent from the very beginning. When the Gang is deciding which office to pursue, Charlie asks, "What's a comptroller?" Mac responds, "Who gives a shit, Dude? We're doing it for the bribe." Dennis is similarly focused on his own enjoyment. Although he accepts Mac's nomination, as soon as the thrill of entering the race wears off, Dennis drops out.

Aristippus would be proud of the Gang's machinations—if not of their lack of success—for he, too, was a spendthrift who desired money to obtain pleasures. In fact, for Aristippus, money was superior to knowledge. According to one anecdote, the Greek tyrant Dionysius I of Syracuse rewarded Plato with a book and Aristippus with a coin. When someone admonished Aristippus for preferring the coin to the book, Aristippus replied, "What would you have? I need money, Plato needs books." The philosopher frequently used his wit for monetary gain. At one point, he begged Dionysius for money. When Dionysius asked, "Did you not but yesterday tell me that a wise man has no want of money?" "Give me the money," replied Aristippus, "and I promise we can settle this question." Dionysius handed over the money, and Aristippus observed, "Now, I am in no want of money."

At the end of the day, the Gang is like Aristippus in spirit, if not success. Dennis, Mac, Charlie, Dee, and Frank are concerned with finding a quick and easy path to pleasure. Hard work is, well, hard, and it detracts from maximizing their pleasure in the moment. Unsurprisingly, the Gang's reluctance to put in effort now to earn rewards in the future is actually limiting their happiness. They jump from scheme to scheme in the hopes of attaining immediate pleasure and ultimately attain nothing but disappointment and unhappiness.

Do You Want to Experience the Experience Machine?

Unfortunately for the Gang, what they think will bring them happiness and what actually will bring them happiness are two very different things. Simply put, hedonism gets it all wrong. Pleasure is good, but it surely can't be the only good worth pursuing. And you don't have to pop some intelligence pills to see why—that is unless you're Charlie ("Flowers for Charlie").

Consider the following thought experiment first developed by the philosopher Robert Nozick in *Anarchy, State, and Utopia*. Suppose there exists an Experience Machine that can give you untold pleasures. This machine works by stimulating electrodes in your brain to simulate any activity you desire. The machine can make you think and feel like you are banging the Waitress that you love, or like you are taking a wonderful road trip to the Grand Canyon, or even like you are eating human meat to satiate your deep, intense craving ("Mac and Dennis: Manhunters"). Whatever your desires, the Experience Machine can provide.

In fact, the machine is so advanced that you will truly believe the experiences are happening to you. In reality, your body will be floating in a tank, with nothing more than electrodes attached to your brain. But you will be unaware of this fact. A scientist approaches you and asks if you want to plug into the machine for the rest of your life. What do you say?

Anyone who subscribes to the hedonist philosophy is committed to plugging in and doing so enthusiastically. If pleasure is the highest good and experiencing pleasure is the sole goal of human life, then the Experience Machine offers the path to the best possible life. After all, no other method would allow you to experience such intense pleasure for so long. Having the opportunity to plug into the Experience Machine is a hedonist's dream come true.

If you are anything like most people, you have a very different response than the hedonist. You would probably decline the scientist's offer and refuse to plug in. But why? Isn't there something undeniably appealing about experiencing your deepest desires for the rest of your life?

Nozick offers several explanations for why the Experience Machine would fail to attract users. First, people want to actually achieve their goals, not just have the experience of achieving them. Second, Nozick observes that being in the machine is "a kind of suicide." You become nothing more than an "indeterminate blob" floating in water. We have strong desires to be a certain type of person and the empty husk in the tank is no type of person anyone would want to be. Finally, Nozick points out that people want to have contact with reality; they do not want to experience a mere simulation of it. At our cores, we want to be connected to some world that is deeper and more important than a manmade simulation.

The Paradox of Hedonism

The Gang's philosophy of "no restrictions" has not played out well. Instead of living in luxury and enjoying every moment, the members of the Gang are frequently left lamenting their lives. Their drive to experience pleasure only backfires and leaves them even unhappier.

Through their struggles, the Gang has fallen subject to the paradox of hedonism. The more you pursue happiness and pleasure, the harder it is to find. But if you redirect your efforts to other activities, happiness will find you. Quite simply, pleasure cannot be achieved directly. As John Stuart Mill wrote:

> Those only are happy . . . who have their minds fixed on some object other than their own happiness. . . . Ask yourself whether you are happy, and you cease to be so.

The Gang is constantly fixated on pleasure. When they act, it is with the goal of obtaining pleasure. However, as Mill observes, this is a clear prescription for failure. Mill is not alone in his conclusions.

The politician William Bennett once likened happiness to a cat: "If you try to coax it or call it, it will avoid you; it will never come. But if you pay no attention to it and go about your business, you'll find it rubbing against your legs and jumping into your lap." The literal part of this advice would have helped Charlie in his quest to recover a cat that had become trapped inside Dee's apartment wall ("Mac and Dennis Break Up"). Instead of bashing a hole in Dee's wall and sending in another cat to lure it out, Charlie could have relaxed and let the cat come to him.

The metaphorical part of the advice, however, is even more useful for the Gang. Instead of pursuing pleasure directly, they should step back and let pleasure come to them. Despite its initial allure, hedonism turns out to be a poor philosophy. It would be wise to learn from the Gang's mistakes.

If you want to be happy, stop pursuing happiness. Focus on other ends, and happiness will come to you.

3
Charlie Gets Beatified

CHRISTOPHER KETCHAM

Forget the episode "The Gang Exploits a Miracle," this newly rediscovered lost episode is the holiest of holies: "Charlie Gets Beatified."

To guide us in reviewing this most blessed plot we will be consulting, as you've probably guessed, the work of the thirteenth-century Franciscans, Peter John Olivi (1248–1298), and the *Doctor Subtilis*, John Duns Scotus (1265–1308). Olivi, you will recall, was admonished for his purported heretical writing and many of his works were banned posthumously by the church. Pope John Paul II made Scotus a saint.

Granted it will be difficult to gain the same honor for Charlie, but never say never. Excommunication or censure is the more likely result for Charlie, now isn't it?

Both Scotus and Olivi were masters of the philosophy of religion. Scotus was famous for his defense of the immaculate conception of the Virgin Mary, and Olivi was infamous for his call for the strictest asceticism, translated: poverty for Franciscans, and this what got him into trouble. But neither will help us make the miracles and other requirements that will encourage the Archdiocese of Philadelphia to begin the canonization process of Charlie beginning with the investigation of him as a Servant of God and then on to the second step: beatification.

Contingency by Aristotle

It's all about contingency and contingency begets free will. Free will is what *It's Always Sunny* is all about. The Gang and its individual members show us that anything that could be possible is possible. They also show us that everything is contingent—meaning that at any moment when you expect someone on the show to do something one way, likely they will do the opposite. Technically this passes for good comedy; good parody. But what is your definition of good? Pretty warped if you think it's the antics performed by the Gang.

But who gave the Gang license for such frolics? Of course, we can say it's the First Amendment to the Constitution of the United States:

> Congress shall make no law respecting an establishment of religion, or prohibiting the free exercise thereof; or abridging the freedom of speech, or of the press; or the right of the people peaceably to assemble, and to petition the Government for a redress of grievances.

But we need to dig a bit deeper and consider a cosmological explanation, the first cause of such a right to be or not to be . . . funny, that is.

We want to get Charlie beatified, the second step on the way to sainthood. But we've a long way to go to get there! We will first figure out what free will is and then move on to God. I told you we were going back in the scheme of things, way back. Remember, God's supposed to be omniscient and omnipotent. God's also supposed to be good and benevolent. With me so far? Aristotle begins the thinking on this.

Aristotle thought that if things *must be* they are a *necessity*, like God. But there's a problem here. Atheists deny that God has ever existed. So humanity is not yet in agreement that God is a necessity. Hmmm. Atheism is not something that good Franciscans in the Middle Ages would have spent too much time debating; but they would have expended considerable effort to develop one elaborate proof after another of God's existence.

Of course, there was the inquisition in Scotus's and Olivi's time, for those who are branded as heretics, but that's long gone. To move forward then in this discussion we must back carefully off the atheism ledge.

Aristotle thought that people like Charlie could be contingent—he *could* or *could not* be. But Aristotle said contingency applies only if Charlie could or could not be at a different moment in time! He thought that if Charlie *is* at this moment then he contingently *could not not be* at this same moment. As a result Aristotle defines contingency as change over time. For Aristotle it is not contingently possible at this moment that Charlie is alive that he could also be dead. And by this explanation Charlie cannot be contingently beatified and, well like he is today, at the same time. But before we move from Aristotle to Scotus and Olivi, we must digress into the world of angels.

Angels Are All the Rage in MCCXLI

You remember the profound question on everyone's lips in 1241, "Did fallen angels sin at the moment of their creation?" This positively divine query overshadowed the news in that year of the last battle of the Mongol invasion of Europe, the succession of Pope Gregory IX by Pope Celestine IV, the murder of Icelandic saga writer Snorri Sturluson by Gissur Þorvaldsson, and the signing of the Treaty of Gwerneigron, following Henry III of England's invasion of Wales. . . . Get me out of this fast!

Hold on, there is a point to this.

More than a good millennium after Aristotle, Scotus had other ideas. To explain how will could be free Scotus used a simple thought experiment. Say Charlie's Angel existed for an instant—came from nothing then disappeared into nothing almost immediately. So far so good. Now, there are good and bad angels. The question is whether Charlie's instant angel could be either good or bad. If an angel could not choose to be good or bad and is simply ordained as such by God, then Charlie's angel can't have free will because it is a necessity that his angel be what God dictates. But if Charlie's angel has free will it could choose to be good or bad in the instant that it exists.

Aristotle thought that something could be contingent only if opposites could occur at another time. But the momentary angel has no other time, only now. So the only way something can be truly contingent is if both opposites are available at the moment of decision. And if Charlie's angel has a contingent decision to make, his angel has free will. We, of course, are hoping that Charlie's angel does have free will and will choose the hallowed route which will lead his earthly minion towards beatification, but we are likely to be disabused of this aspiration by the writers of the show. You see the road to beatification for Charlie is strewn with boulders, gullies, and washouts.

Scotus versus Aristotle

For Scotus, at this moment while Charlie is alive, he could also be dead. He isn't, of course, but he could be. Why did many of his contemporaries think Scotus's idea was better than Aristotle's? Actually it comes down to God and free will.

If God created the universe and makes everything happen according to a single strict recipe, nothing could be contingent. We would be automatons in God's play. Free will would not be possible because we would be destined forever to do exactly what God had planned for us. Where's the fun in that? And do we really believe that the most benevolent God would be directing Charlie to perform his wild antics? We would ask, "For what purpose does God do this?" and smite ourselves all over with nettles and switches and wail and howl in protest.

Scotus pointed out that something may be immutable, meaning *it must be*—but something that's immutable *does not have to be* a necessity. While for Scotus God is an immutable necessity, contingency is immutable but not a necessity. Meaning that God created contingency but that contingency does not have to be possible, say in a different universe, or if God abolished contingency in this one. And God created this universe, but God didn't have to.

So to keep God a necessity and omniscient and omnipotent *and* make it so humans have free will in God's universe, what has to happen? Scotus's idea was to say that God the necessity has "immutable knowledge of our *contingent* future." So God created contingency which God could eliminate at any moment, but with contingency God also created our will. God created our will, "but has endowed it with something of his own freedom, giving it the special power to determine itself." So Scotus saved the omniscient omnipotent God by giving God infinite knowledge. But because God also created contingency and God gave us free will, Charlie can get beatified or not. What was God thinking?

The Miracle of Water into Wine

The bar 10:20 P.M. Frank, Dennis, Charlie and Mac are there. Frank pops his head up from a slouch on a barstool.

FRANK: Charlie, I want you off my couch and out of the apartment. . . . We need a plan, Gang.

DENNIS: Well, sometimes, you know, he speaks like in tongues. Let's get him beatified. Then he can go live in a rectory or something.

FRANK: I'm listening. So, how do we get Charlie beatified? Is that like getting beaten really hard?

MAC: No, it's the stuff the Catholic Church does when you are on the way to sainthood. Just takes a miracle. Loaves into fishes, cure blindness, lower cholesterol.

CHARLIE: Oh, not another Virgin Mary miracle.

FRANK: Charlie as a saint. I'm buyin it! Maybe a miracle that would be more tavern-like. How about . . . How about . . . Why not water into wine?

MAC: Okay, how do you do that? [*Frank shrugs.*]

FRANK: I got it. Here. [*Fills a beer glass from the glass cleaning sink. The others frown.*] Got a better idea? Use this red food die to make it look like wine. Where's Deidra? Oh Deidra. Dee!

DEE: What? [*from inside the rest room*]

FRANK: [*shouting*] We want to make sure you're in on this miracle. Charlie's gonna turn water into wine.

DEE: [*comes out of the rest room*] I gotta see this. [*walks over to the bar*]

FRANK: You're gonna prove that it's wine.

DEE: Okay, how's that?

FRANK: By drinking it, dummy. Here—see it's water. [*Holds up the glass filled with soapy water*]

DEE: Ewww.

FRANK: Naw. Not this. Remember it becomes wine after Charlie zaps the miracle on it.

[*Frank gives Charlie the glass and waives his hands over it and secretly dribbles in the food coloring. Charlie swirls the glass around.*]

FRANK: Ta Da. [*Hands the glass to Dee*]

DEE: It doesn't look like wine. It's got a head on it.

FRANK: It's Champagne.

DEE: It's red.

FRANK: You never heard of pink Champagne?

DEE: It's still red.

FRANK: It's Pink Champagne of the red grape variety.

[*Dee takes a sip and retches loudly. The Gang gets Dee very drunk. She records a slurring and rambling selfie of Charlie's miracle of turning water into wine. The miracle's done and recorded.*]

Now back to that thing about free will. Where were we?

Necessities Neschmessities

So Scotus had to meditate on how to get out of this Aristotelian mess without demoting God and elevating Humans. The right balance of being—God and Human must be sought. How many states of being are there? Well, first there is *necessity*, which is something that is true in all possible worlds. The word *gang* requires more than one member to be part of the episode or there would not be a gang. This is a *necessity*, always true in any possible "gang" world. Now we could have one member on the set and another on the phone or even hold a gangathon chat over the internet, but it takes two for there to be a Gang.

On the other hand, *contingent* means something that's true in at least one possible world. While at least two members of the gang must be in the same episode, what is contingent is which members. Not every episode has to have every Gang member present and accounted for. If we get Charlie beatified he may quit this earthly Gang altogether for something more ethereal besides huffing glue. Then there is the *impossibility*. I know what you're going to say: anything to do with reality in *It's Always Sunny* is an impossibility. But get this, in Season One Frank was not even part of the Gang yet. So, in Season One Frank was not a possible player in the show nor could he have possibly been a member of the gang. In Season One, Frank was an *impossibility*.

Living the Contingent Life Necessarily

There are times in the series where there is both necessity and contingency. You are led to necessity by your nose ring right into the depths with the gang. There is no contingent option. Straight down into the wormhole (not the *Star Trek* kind, the kind with real worms.) In the episode "Gun Fever," there is no choice, there is no option, there will be a gun; it will get used. Writing Regulations 101, Section B, Subparagraph 324.5: it is a necessity, a cardinal rule, a categorical imperative, a prime directive that if a gun is mentioned anywhere in the book, short story, script, or play, it must be used, no exception. So the title of the episode lets us know this up front and in the opening scene the bar gets burglarized. . . . There *will* be firearm(s). There is no choice. But we are free to do anything else with the plot once the gun regulation has been satisfied. What becomes contingent after complying with the necessary gun regulation is how the gun is used or abused.

Now, what do you think happens with the gun in this episode? If you said the choices are: purchase one and keep for use only in emergency such as a robbery, target shooting, concealed weapon, robbery, intimidation, personal injury, dating the bar's burglar . . . You would be right on all counts. So the gun is not contingent but its use is. It's also contingent who gets shot. The gang believes it's Colin who has burglarized the bar at the beginning of the episode and later in the show they see someone in disguise sneaking around the bar. They shoot, but it's Charlie who's trying to steal from the bar. While they are in the hospital attending to Charlie, Colin burglarizes the bar for real.

That's the upshot of Scotus's contingency, it can go either way. But you're right, the gang can go only one way—to the murky side.

A Medieval Gang Gets Contingent

As we know from watching *It's Always Sunny* over the years, everything's contingent. While Scotus was fleshing out his theory of contingency he likely read Olivi's writing about free will. Olivi probably gave Scotus a clue to how he could solve the problem of contingency.

Olivi said that there are seven attitudes pairs (one attitude pair for each Gang member and some to spare). They include: "Zeal and mercy, friendship and hostility, shame and glory, gratitude and ingratitude, subjugation and domination, hope and distrust, carefulness and heedlessness." So now you see where Scotus got the contingency idea from. . . . Olivi's opposites are juxtaposed against each other and human freedom and free will dictate that both items of each pair be present at the same time.

Olivi likely saw that the Franciscans (his Gang) could be zealous, hostile, glory driven, ungrateful, dominant, distrustful and heedless (why that's our Gang too!). I imagine this is why Olivi wrote so fervently about the need for strict asceticism and poverty for Franciscans. As his censored writing faded into Dark Ages obscurity, Olivi likely did not think it was "Always Sunny in the Holy See."

Grotesque

So you think that there could not have been anything like the Gang in the thirteenth century? Prepare to be enlightened! There was the 'Feast of Fools' and other grotesques and carnivals where lay people greeted each other with abusive language, mocked clerics and carried out all sorts of lewd and blasphemous acts much like our Gang.

So in one feast or another there might be monstrosities and oddities that one would see at a carnival slide show, gluttony, parody, drunkenness and lay person mockeries of lusting, greedy, covetous, and intemperate clergy. Lords greeted serfs and serfs greeted lords and poked fun with bawdy aphorisms . . . but only during the festival. The genre, *Its Always Sunny*, is nothing new. In fact, we might even blush today if treated with the downright vulgarity of this Middle Ages version of vaudeville and slapstick that occurred during the Feast of Fools.

We wonder sometimes whether the gang could ever have both of each of Olivi's attitude pairs because it almost seems that it is a necessity for the Gang or one of its members to make the daftest decision. But this is not always the case because sometimes a logical decision by one member of the Gang sets the rest off in the intemperate direction. In the episode "Gun Fever Too: Still Hot," Frank goes on a television news show to tout guns, Gunther's guns. The rest of the gang see Frank's bit and begin a "hot" gun debate: more guns; less guns. Dennis and Dee first want guns off the street and go hunting for guns to show how easy they are to get. They get burned in a gun sale and now want more guns.

Charlie and Mac think there aren't enough guns and set about to become gun-toting vigilantes at a middle school. They bring middle-school students back to the bar to give them survivalist training but this backfires and Charlie and Mac reverse their positions and now want guns off the street. But at the end of the show Frank chimes in to the rest of the gang that the whole thing about guns was a ruse. He had no interest in guns, he only had an interest in Gunther's guns where he had taken an ownership stake. See, Frank's decision to go on the air to tout guns wasn't daft—it was just business.

In fact the genius of this series is that it folds back in upon itself and its double entendre plots go a long way to proving that not only do these idiots have free will but also whatever you or I might do they probably won't. In the strangest and most perverse way, the gang proves Scotus and Olivi right!

Wouldn't the most bizarre episode ever be the Gang sitting around the bar in banal conversation where nothing untoward happens? Would you be throwing empties at the screen and screaming, "Gimme my money back", or would you be glued to the tube in anticipation of the moment when pleasantries will suddenly dissolve? Think about it, wouldn't you look back at this as the most perverse of all the shows in the series because the characters had become positively demented in their stupefied crossing over to the light side? But there's always the possibility of that happening, isn't there?

The Gang proves that there is contingency because the Gang itself is contingent, capable of doing one thing and its opposite within the same show as in "Gun Fever Too: Still Hot!" Sure, they lack conviction. And that will be the most difficult problem to overcome to get Charlie beatified. He's got to get into the right habit.

A Beatification Update

Sorry, but the Gang's been incarcerated, even Charlie. Of course they did—try to exploit the miracle of water into wine, that is. They changed the name of the tavern to the "Miracle Pub, formerly Paddy's." To get more patrons and donations to their "miracle fund," they thought it would be cool to post handbills all over Broad Street where the Philadelphia Flyers were playing the New York Rangers the previous night. The handbill invited fans of both teams to come to "See the Believers in Bondage at the Miracle Pub . . . first two beers free." That night half of the Gang was dressed in Ranger jerseys and half in Flyers jerseys. Each member of the Gang was equipped with bondage gear like whips and chains. The idea was to get patrons to whip and otherwise abuse either of two mannequin "saints" guarding the shrine, one wearing a Ranger's jersey and the other a Flyers jersey. Their plan was to charge a buck donation for each whipping.

Before the end of the game a bunch of elderly women showed up at the bar to see the shrine. While the Gang was trying to get money out of the women and get them out of the bar before the fans showed up, . . . the fans showed up. Well, you guessed it. Mayhem. Fights, fire, sprinklers discharging, elder abuse, assault, battery, ambulances, police, fire officials, street closing, yellow tape, and off to jail in handcuffs, fans and gang members alike.

Another setback for beatification. But there's still time. This script says there's a Part Two. . . . We're hoping that Charlie takes time in the slammer to pen a most beatific redemption treatise. You know he won't. But he could.

II

Psychology

4
What's So Creepy about Unibrows and Incest?

Charlene Elsby

The Gang, from some perspectives, behaves often blasphemously, offensively, narcissistically, or in other ways not conducive to what we might think are proper social relations. But there's something distinctive about the creepiness of the McPoyles that lets us say that the Gang isn't quite *there* yet.

The characters in the Gang function well enough within society—they have jobs, know people, and so forth, and though they often act based on a non-standard interpretation of what's going on around them, they don't yet reach the status of irredeemable creeps. The McPoyles, on the other hand, seem to embody that irredeemable creepiness in everything they do.

We don't really know what they're doing in between their run-ins with the Gang, but I'm pretty sure they don't have a league-ranking bridge team or hold down day jobs at the bank. They have successfully crossed the line into creepiness which makes them something distinct, almost incomprehensible, something outside the bounds of civil society that creeps in every so often, throwing rocks from the edge of society towards the fringes (which is where the Gang seems to hang out).

Mc-Frickin'-Poyles

The McPoyles and their activities range anywhere from slightly disturbing to vomit-inducing. Only in their first appearance do they seem to be anywhere within the bounds of societal norms, in the brief flashback to one year ago, when they were drinking with Charlie, at which time Charlie suggested they claim their former gym teacher molested them and sue the school board for millions.

In that one shot they seem to be out on the town, having a lovely time. But this is early in the development of the McPoyles. The first time we see Liam McPoyle, we know something's not quite right. Charlie stops by to tell the McPoyles they can't, in actuality, sue the school board, because that's completely unacceptable (he says they're going to Hell). "We considered that," says Ryan McPoyle.

The threat doesn't seem to faze him, and I doubt it's because he's a devout atheist who has developed a series of rational arguments against the possibility of eternal damnation. He's simply weighed the risks and decided it doesn't matter. But even just as Charlie arrives, something's off. Liam doesn't even know how to invite someone in correctly. He invites him in, but he doesn't get out of the way. There's a missing connection there between what needs to be accomplished (Charlie getting in the house) and what needs to be done to accomplish that (providing a necessary path to do so). There's some logical connection missing in both of these deductions that makes them seem just a little *off*.

It's questionable, at times, whether the *off*-ness of the McPoyles is deliberate or not. In "Charlie Goes America All Over Everybody's Ass," Liam McPoyle reverses the burden of defining what constitutes deviant behavior back on society, claiming, "It's society that has the problem." While some believe that certain values are subjective, or culturally relative, there remains that creepiness factor that screams at us that the McPoyles are not simply making other, non-standard life choices, but doing something wrong—that there is a correct way of doing things, and they're not doing it right.

Where does that feeling of creepiness come from? Let's look closely at some examples.

Bathrobes

The McPoyles like their bathrobes. It's all bathrobes, all the time. When they take the gang hostage in "The Gang Gets Held Hostage," they force their bathrobe ideals on their hostages. I like bathrobes too, but not in a creepy way.

What's the problem with bathrobes in public? The McPoyle sense of style is both comfortable and practical. Granted, they look like they could use a wash, but we can't hold that against bathrobes in general. But we look at the McPoyles in their bathrobes and get a sense that something's *off.*

What's going on? Manners of appropriate dress for public appearances are conventional, certainly. There is a way to dress for certain events, in certain places, with certain people. Showing up to a casual event in a fancy dress will get you a couple of odd stares, but these will lean more towards pitying your misinterpretation of the dress code than a reaction to your creepiness. If you wear a bathrobe to a bar, on the other hand, we're all going to be thinking to ourselves, "Oh my god, I can't believe you're wearing the wrong amalgamation of fabrics to this establishment, at this time of day."

Bathrobes are for the house, for when you're in between stages of appropriate dress. Sure, there are some perfectly all-right outfits that closely resemble bathrobes (I'm thinking wrap dresses here), but the difference seems to be clear. If you're obviously wearing a bathrobe outside, you've either been locked out while getting the newspaper (which is not cool, but still acceptable), or there's something wrong with you. We don't know what that something is, but we don't like it. Somehow, you've failed to realize what everybody else has realized: bathrobes are for home use only. And your failure to realize that means that something's gotten lost in that creepy little head of yours in between your getting dressed and daring to go outside in that ratty old thing.

The failure to meet the social convention of appropriate dress works on a sliding scale. There's accidental deviation, through ignorance or something like that (the invitation didn't specify no bowties required), and then there's flouting the rules like you just don't care. And *then*, there's flouting the rules because you didn't even know there was such a thing as a convention. Nothing breaks into the thought process of "Gee, my bathrobe is comfy," and "I think I'll go out for a bit," where normally something would break through, like, "What is it appropriate to be seen in out there?"

We get a sense that something is lacking in that logic when we see somebody who unabashedly wanders about in their sleepwear. Something is *off*, and there are two possible reactions we can have to this outsider: peck it to death like a deformed chicken, or get the fuck away. With the McPoyles, I think we get a little bit of both.

Is this really justified, though? Who am I to say that your choice in fabric shapes is inappropriate? (Let's assume everything important is covered, since to assume otherwise would open up a whole other discussion of what's "appropriate".) There is some kind of conventional association between what you are and aren't allowed to wear, and what we're used to seeing either in public or in private situations. But if I want to wear Popeye pyjamas while I'm at the laundromat, who's really going to care?

Unibrows

> You know, your eyebrow drives me crazy. It's so thick. It's so dark, so very connected. You're a stone-cold fox, Margaret. You're a stone-cold fox, and I want you.

So says Dennis to Margaret McPoyle in "The Gang Gets Held Hostage." The McPoyle unibrow is also prominently featured (get it?) in "The Maureen Ponderosa Wedding Massacre," where we see the rest of the McPoyles (at least, the strains of the bloodline that weren't lost to syphilis or mongoloidism). Part of the creepiness of the McPoyles is their physical appearance. Bathrobes aside, the McPoyle clan aren't exactly what we'd call the most attractive lot.

This brings out an important observation about the relation between ugliness and creepiness. The McPoyles as characters are obviously made up in such a way as to detract from the appearances of the actors who play them. When creating these creepy characters, someone made a conscious decision to make them ugly. It's a pretty common thing, too. I'm confident in saying that in movie representations, the ugly people tend to be portrayed as the more villainous, less sympathetic, and, in this case, creepy.

There are certain physical traits which are generally considered ugly. Barring any discussion of cultural relevance (the McPoyles are portrayed as existing in *this* culture, where unibrows are generally not accepted as the hottest thing to have), physical appearance is often linked to character traits. The whole discipline of physiognomy, for instance, attempted to justify judging someone based on their physical attributes in order to infer character traits: so-and-so has a witty nose, a barbarous forehead, or an overindulgent chin.

What I'm saying is that society tends to judge people on physical appearance. Tall people tend to be perceived as more competent (see, for instance, Young and French on height and the perceived competence of US presidents). When the physical characteristic is something that the person has control over, the judgments only get more pronounced. Not only is someone worse for having a physical trait, it's their own damn fault. The whole contemporary concept of "fat-shaming" is just such a thing. Another thing is the McPoyle unibrow. What's running through the head of the person judging these people is "Why don't you just go pluck it?" Now there are two levels to how society is judging these people: 1. they're ugly; 2. they're not even fulfilling the basic human obligation of *doing something about it.*

Why aren't they doing something about it? There are a few possible reasons. One would be that their perception is all messed up, that the "Beauty is in the eye of the beholder" thing has resulted in the McPoyles believing that unibrows are cool. But this isn't the immediate conclusion of the average person beholding them. Rather, there must be something off.

Either Margaret McPoyle is so incompetent that she can't even pluck an eyebrow, or she's given up on gainful social interaction and just doesn't give a fuck. Both of these options creep us out. The societal outsider doesn't act in accordance with how we might expect them to, and therefore creeps us out. The complete incompetent can't be expected to have the wherewithal to follow the social rules we've established, and they therefore also creep us out. Essentially, we can't predict the behavior of someone with such a thick, bushy unibrow, and we perceive that as a problem. Maybe it's society that has the problem, maybe not.

Incest

The incestuous relationships between the McPoyles are something we learn about the McPoyles right at the start, or at least they're hinted at when in "Charlie Got Molested," Charlie goes to the McPoyles' house and Liam explains that Ryan isn't downstairs yet because, "We just got out of the shower." The fact that the McPoyles have sex with each other is immediately revolting. The Gang thinks so too (see their reactions in "The Gang Gets Held Hostage"). This is the reaction we as the audience expect, and it's the one we get. Does society have the problem in this case?

Both Charles Darwin and Albert Einstein married their first cousins, to whom they were also related in other ways. So how close is too close? In North American marriage laws, for instance, it's pretty standard to forbid marrying your sisters, brothers, parents, grandparents, children, and grandchildren. (There's still a debate about cousins.) There are some biological arguments for and against incest. The whole point of banning incestuous relationships, according to the common understanding, is that inbreeding causes deformities and other health issues for the offspring. But there's another line of reasoning that concludes that by inbreeding, the characteristic traits of the bloodline become amplified or exaggerated. Sure, there's a deformity every now and then, but it's also possible to concentrate some genetic trait by selectively breeding individuals with the same traits—and who's more like you than family?

This is where, I think, the creepiness argument comes from. People often say that incest is creepy *because* it's a natural reaction to the inevitably deformed children that result from such a union. The other line of reasoning says *it's just fucking creepy*. Like pedophiles, the incestuous are an example of something gone wrong that's going to harm the rest of us and must be stopped and severely punished. But unlike with pedophiles, we kind of just have to sit back and be grossed out 'cause, hey, consenting adults.

The creepiness of the McPoyles' incest might be rationalized in the following way: what we're looking at is a severely fucked up family with a misguided belief that their incestuous relationships are keeping the bloodline pure, and we know it's misguided because they are *that fucked up* ("The Maureen Ponderosa Wedding Massacre"). They have the same reaction to Liam marrying an outsider that we do to his brother blowing him. Is this a morally relative thing? The fact that there *are* people who do that doesn't mean yes. There are a lot of strange people around, and we certainly feel like we have the right to judge them. On the practical side, at least they're not running around trying to pick up chicks on the internet all creepy-like. They've got their dating pool on a Local Area Network.

Milk

The McPoyles drink a lot of milk. Now that doesn't sound like anything in and of itself. It's possible you know someone who's all about the milk, and don't think there's anything wrong with that. Maybe they work out a lot. It's the protein, you know.

When the McPoyles do it, though, it just seems weird. Maybe it's because there are so many of them—it's okay to have one weird uncle who drinks a lot of milk, but all of them? They're kind of turning it into a thing. That is, the consistency with which they do it and the fact that the milk thing is a common feature to the McPoyles starts to make you wonder: What's with the milk? And then there's the inference: That's kind of creepy. I think that in the McPoyles' case, the milk thing is creepy for all of the reasons that bathrobes, unibrows, and incest are creepy.

First, there's the fact that they drink milk *all the time*. You just don't order milk at a bar. But the McPoyles do. It's as inappropriate as wearing a bathrobe to a bar. And they do both at once. It's the same lack of awareness of context they're demonstrating here. There are certain modes of dress you come to expect from people at different times in different places, and there are certain beverages associated with different times and different places: coffee (or mimosas) at breakfast, beer at a bar. But milk, *all the time*? There's something odd about that.

Then there's the idea that it just seems unnatural to consume so much milk. What trait have they evolved where they can (or maybe have to?) drink so much milk? There's something odd about that. Perhaps the milk is the only thing keeping the bloodline alive, some basic flaw in the system that can only be mitigated by vast milk consumption. What's with that?

Another theory I'd consider is that it's really just a matter of taste. There's nothing wrong with it at all, but the fact that the McPoyles do so many other creepy things just makes it seem as if this must also be creepy, because everything they do is creepy. To think that they do a single normal thing would throw off our perception of them as all-around creeps, so it's just easier to fit the milk thing onto the list of creepy things than it would be to consider that hey, maybe the milk thing is just fine. (A philosopher would call that an inductive inference). Or maybe the milk drinking is really creepy, and that weird uncle who drinks a lot of milk but seems otherwise fine is just on a slippery slope to full-on creepdom.

On the other hand, it's all too easy to envision the McPoyles gleefully suckling fresh milk from a poor unsuspecting cow (who's probably also a McPoyle). I'll leave you with that image.

So what *is* the essence of creepiness? Is it the weird feeling you get when creepy people are around, or is it the people themselves? And what about the creepy people who don't give off the creep vibe? (There's always that guy who looks normal, acts normal, but in the end turns out to eat people's faces for brunch.) I'd like to say it's one of those "You know it when you see it" things, but sometimes you miss it. And then there are those people who seem creepy, but turn out to be okay. (Do you remember Old Man Marley from *Home Alone*?)

Creepiness detection is more of an art than a science. Whether someone *is* creepy is a different question from whether they *seem* creepy. The projected creep contributes to your perception of creepiness, but so do your individual experiences and beliefs. So if you meet a creepy person, give them a chance. And if they're still creepy, run. You can't tell what those creeps are up to.

5
Psychoanalyzing the Game of Games

Daniel Leonard

It's not always sunny in Philadelphia. This is a meteorological fact. According to the NOAA, the City of Brotherly Love averages over 110 "partially cloudy days" each year—days when clouds cover one-fourth to three-fourths of the sky. In fact, only ninety-three days a year can be described as "sunny." Sunlight reaches the ground in Philly only fifty-six percent of the time between sunrise and sunset. There's precipitation 119 days a year. And we all know it rains on the Gang's parade more than most.

So why claim otherwise? Visual hallucination? Pathological lying? Wishful thinking? All of the above?

The false title of the show gets at something fundamental about its main characters: they're all masters of self-deception. They fool themselves into rehearsing the same schemes and routines over and over, expecting something to change. But how do they manage this so consistently? Why are their lives such wrecks? What's wrong with them? The answers lie in one of the Gang's longest-running routines—the game CharDee MacDennis.

The Gang Exposes Its Deep-Seated Desires

The basics:

- To win CharDee MacDennis, be the first team to complete (in order) all three levels: Mind, Body, and Spirit.

- To complete a level, collect a certain number of cards by succeeding in or winning challenges.

- Between levels, engage in civil conversation.

- The penalty for breaching a rule or failing in a challenge is forced drinking. The type of alcohol progresses in each level, from wine to beer to spirits.

- If a team catches another team cheating, the first team advances either one level or to the level of the cheating team, whichever is higher.

- If the fifteen-minute time limit is reached and the teams are tied, decide a winner by drawing the Black Card.

- Winners may smash losers' game pieces.

- Questions about gameplay may not be asked during the game.

The game aims to judge which players are superior to their foes in mind, body, and spirit. Dee and Dennis, who have won the game all nineteen times it's been played, believe it judges effectively; they only allow Frank to play because "Frank's mind is still very strong, but his body's very, very weak, so I think it's a wash," plus "his spirit's garbage" (about which Frank agrees). So the game must reflect the Gang's notion of what well-developed faculties would be like. To figure out what's so messed-up about their portrayal of personhood, let's get help from the twentieth century's most famous philosopher of self, Sigmund Freud (1856–1939).

Freud, the Viennese founder of psychoanalysis, is famous—and infamous—for ideas like "the Oedipus complex," "the death drive," "the unconscious," "libido," "free association," "transference," "infantile sexuality," and "wish fulfillment."

Late in his life, he developed a three-part "structural model" of the human psyche. In English, the parts are usually called by Latin names: id, ego, and superego. To translate Freud's German more directly, they're the It, the I, and the Over-I.

Simply put, the id is the source of unconscious, unreasoning, selfish impulses and drives (Charlie: "Wildcard, Bitches!"). The superego offers criticism learned from others, especially culture and parents (Frank, to Dee: "It's not your fault, Sweetie. You're just not pretty enough"). The ego mediates between both of those extremes in order to deal with reality (for lack of a better example, Dee: "The problem is: I'm gonna have a really hard time if we're both cannibals *and* we're racists"). So what does CharDee MacDennis's first level—called "Mind"—have to do with the Freudian model of the mind?

Mind: I Don't If You Don't

The Mind level supposedly includes "Trivia, Puzzles, and Artistry." But none of the "trivia" questions are about facts— they're really about remembering the arbitrary matters of opinion the Gang had cared about when they created the game and then repeating the answers they'd written on a whim. For instance, Charlie draws a card with a question he wrote himself: "Denis is asshole. Y Charlee hat?" The correct answer (which Charlie no longer remembers, but Dennis does) is, "Becauze Denis is a bastardt man." Charlie recounts to Dennis the simple explanation for this card: "I was mad at you about something." The "trivia" gives importance to what had been a minor—that is, trivial—annoyance, expressing it as unbridled hatred and memorializing it for years to come. This has everything to do with id.

The id is the part of a person that simply *wants*. It's a mishmash of needs and desires, and it seeks instant gratification of all of them. In a sense, it's the part of you that's impersonal (hence "the It"): it begins in you before you're born, and it takes no heed of your thoughts or observations. All it wants to do is release the tension of not yet having its demands met. Freud names the id's guiding rule "the Pleasure

Principle": avoid unpleasure. Unpleasure is the sensation when the instinctual energy in the id, which Freud names "libido," meets an obstacle. He envisions the id as "that great reservoir of libido"—and it wants, like a dammed river, to flow. With lines like, "I'm gonna chop a piece of that fat little calf muscle of yours and I'm gonna eat it!" (Charlie to Frank, in "Mac and Dennis: Manhunters"), the Gang lets id-impulses determine its actions to an obscene extent.

We don't get to see the "Puzzles" part of the "Mind" level, but the "Artistry" component is just as id-based as the trivia. While one teammate draws a picture on the other's back, the other must determine what idea is depicted, "based solely on feel." The answer is "kicking"—a physical gesture. Charlie and Frank guess correctly not because of drawing skill, but because of their "stupid, strange connection with each other." There's no subtlety or critical consideration involved; this is really a test of the Gang's receptivity to physical stimulation and ability to 'go with their gut.' The id consists of bodily drives, including erotic impulses (close friends touching and feeling each other in the game, and even Charlie's "strange connection" with his probable biological father) and aggressive urges (the Charlie-hates-Dennis card, Dennis's anger about Dee's bony back, the kicking). The Gang's psychology is so backwards that the "Mind" level of their game involves precisely what *isn't* part of the conscious mind.

The id has a big problem: its demands are unrealistic. The pleasure Charlie gets from sniffing glue, paint, and cleaning fluids keeps him from achieving the greater pleasure of getting the Waitress into bed. In the "Mind" level of Chardee MacDennis, both Mac's lie about the "Mind" level's "Chance" card and its real content—"Take the money from everyone's pockets" and "Swallow this card whole"—present an occasion for satisfying brutal lusts without regard for long-term consequences like incarceration and indigestion. (Many real-world games, from Bloody Knuckles to Spin the Bottle, do likewise.) Such consequences typically foil the Gang's impulsive plans at every corner, leaving them more unhappy than when they started. For instance, when Dennis, Mac, and Frank remake Paddy's Pub as an "anything-goes" bar, it has the side effect of attracting their enemies (the McPoyles) to the bar. Meanwhile, Charlie gets stabbed and a man dies in Frank's gambling-ring game of Russian Roulette ("Charlie Goes America All Over Everybody's Ass"). To avoid situations like these and find longer-lasting satisfaction, the Gang needs to take its game to the next level.

Body: You Gotta Pay the Control Toll

The "Body" level—surprise!—isn't really about the body. The so-called "Mind" level already covered impulsive physical behavior, so the real topic must be something else. This time, the Gang's original description of the level actually does match the tasks: not flinching while having a dart thrown at one's hand ("Pain"); being locked in a dog kennel while stomaching raw cake ingredients ("Endurance"); and not chewing or swallowing while "gobbling" as many grapes as possible ("Physical Challenge"). The theme is made clear by the additional, non-physical rule added for this level: no cursing. The theme is restraint. In keeping with the Gang's backwardness, restraint is properly the role of the ego, the major player in consciousness—that is, Mind!

The ego is a politician. It tries to appease three conflicting demands all at the same time: the id's thoughtless urges, the superego's perfectionistic criticisms, and reality's limiting conditions. This requires making compromises (only partially satisfying each demand) and telling lies (tricking the id or superego into feeling appeased). To form its plans, the ego takes experience and the external world into account so that we can achieve long-term happiness without having our urges foil us in the meantime. It uses the higher, experience-based mental faculties—memory, perception, reason, common sense—to adapt the id's impulses toward courses of action with a higher probability of success or a greater ultimate payoff. To avoid unpleasant feelings of censure from others or guilt from within, it also tries to choose actions that satisfy the conscience and conform to the behavioral ideals demanded by the superego.

To 'adapt' the id's desires usually involves deferring instant gratification. Since this is a sign of maturity, it's hard to find examples of it among the Gang's actions. For a trivial (and obviously unhealthy) example, Dennis's application of the D.E.N.N.I.S. System for wooing women demands that he put forth a great deal of energy to manipulate a woman over an extended period of time, suffer the stress of coordinating his plans, and take on the risk of having his scheme backfire—all for the sadistic payoff of remaining the object of a woman's desire even as he rejects and abandons her. For a more mature ego, the same effort might be applied to the give-and-take of a healthy marriage. Clearly Dennis is driven by more than merely adjusting for reality. Why, we might ask, is Dennis so driven to coerce women into loving him unconditionally? Did he once suffer traumatic rejection by a parent? In fact, yes: by his biological father, Bruce Mathis.

The Body level shows that all the Gang members' egos are dominated by infantile urges at the expense of being realistic or acting morally. It's the only level of the game that values restraint, yet it only applies to physical tasks. It's true that the prohibition on swearing isn't directly a physical task, but swearing is a secondary form of aggression—it's a siphon for the desire to punch or bite what gets in your way, and swear words almost exclusively refer to sexual and excretory organs and functions. The ability to exert physical self-restraint is crucial in the infantile stages of human development. Babies begin with no restraint at all; in the womb, where all their needs were met without their intervention, they never needed it. As a child ages and must cope with hunger, pain, the parents' occasional absence, unpleasant food, and the need to become potty trained, she begins (hopefully) to develop coping skills. These skills eventually need to be extended to peer relationships, schoolwork, and other stressors that are more emotional than physical. The more a person learns to cope with short-term emotional frustration and pain, the more fulfilled she can become. As Freud puts it, "Where It (the id) was, there I (the ego) shall come to be." But the Gang seems to have stopped somewhere in preschool. Though they sorely lack in maturity of ego, do they make up for it in strength of spirit?

Spirit: Not Even Once

Nope. That's the thing: human spirit *is* maturity of ego—a resilient sense of self. But the tasks the Gang assigns in the Spirit level ("Emotional Battery" and "Public Humiliation") are exactly the ones that turn the focus away from the sense of self and toward the opinions of everyone else. And the way to win this level isn't necessarily to show a strong sense of self; after being berated by the Gang during the previous play-through of the game, Dee "cried for a month straight" and "tried to kill herself." The way to win is simply to consent to being exposed to criticism. Doing so offers the player a chance to internalize the criticism so that he can anticipate the voices of others and avoid displeasing them in the future: the task of the superego.

A person's superego makes use of an "ego ideal," a self one wants to become. This ideal self is assembled from traits of others who have cared for the person, most notably one's father, the archetypal 'provider.' It makes sense to seek to develop these traits so that a person can grow up to be self-sufficient. The attributes of parents are stressed so strongly in the superego because they're the ones who help a person when she is most helpless: as an infant. The behavior instructions one learns from one's parents as an infant involve restraint, as does the ego; but instead of simply postponing satisfaction, the superego demands that satisfaction in certain areas be given up entirely. "Don't touch that! Don't eat that! Don't hit your brother! Don't lie to me! Don't pick your nose!" Certain directives (for instance, the aforementioned ones that forbid lying and nose-picking) don't necessarily pay off with later pleasures for the individual, but simply reflect cultural values—values a civilization deems necessary not for the individual, but for the group. If the id presents one's own disorganized desires to act, the superego presents others' organized inhibitions against certain actions. To counterbalance the pleasure provided by the id, the superego attaches a negative feeling to the actions and intentions it opposes—the feeling of guilt.

Even though Level 3 is interrupted in this episode's playthrough and the tasks aren't performed, the interruptions themselves are excellent manifestations of superego. Frank, the Gang's father-figure, exposes his children's breaking of the game's universal rules (they're drinking water instead of alcohol) and deceit (they're pretending they aren't) so that they will be punished for it. And it's when Dennis fails to restrain his aggression toward his father that he exposes his own rule-breaking; Dennis yells "Shut up, dog!" and throws the contents of his beer bottle in Frank's face, but Frank tastes that it's only water. Perhaps this blunder wasn't a total accident; Dennis may have been driven by an unconscious desire to expose his own behavior so that he'd be found out and punished. Then it would be as if his biological father, the all-seeing vehicle of punishment and justice, had come back.

Can we really say this level represents the superego, when all the critical voices still come from others instead of having been internalized? Yes: this way of getting things backwards shows the Gang members' wishes to reverse the development of their superegos. Despite appearances, the Gang's superegos are *overly* strong. Even though they rarely behave in accordance with social norms, they do routinely rationalize their behavior, overcompensate for perceived shortcomings, and place inordinate value on being liked or accepted by certain people—all signs that they're reacting to an inner voice saying that they need to be better. Their attempts to drown out this voice simply show how loud it is for them without making it any quieter. Their wishful thinking against the superego guided them to create the Black Card, which they draw to decide the winner when the clock runs out. The card's instruction: "And so it comes to this: Flip a coin." It's as if they wish they could say to their superegos:

"See? What happens to me is beyond my control. No matter how hard I try to please you, the vicissitudes of external reality get the better of me. Stop criticizing me, and leave me to pursue my id-urges unhindered. None of my problems are my fault. Shut up, dog!"

Thank You! But Our Father Figure Is in Another Castle!

Despite what the rules say, everyone wins in CharDee MacDennis. Otherwise, why would Mac and Charlie still want to play after having lost so many times? The truth is that simply playing the game gives the whole Gang the chance to identify dissolving the pesky superego with the height of 'Spirit'. Dissolving the superego amounts to returning to a pre-civilized, animalistic state. The voice of conscience is exactly what's kept out of the game; it's confined to the interludes, where it's caricatured as being overly polite and directed toward trivial manners. This is again a wish: the Gang would be willing to tolerate the superego if they only felt guilt about such matters as what to wear and how to hold a wine glass instead of about important issues like how to go about their careers and love lives. None of them has achieved traditional success or stability of any kind, and they're ashamed of it.

The prize for winning the game is an overt enactment of the wish to revert to the id. The winners stomp the losers' game pieces, a symbolic murder—the act prohibited by the superego with the very greatest urgency and strength, since it's the most total realization of the id's primal aggressiveness.

Moreover, the game pieces aren't merely figures of the losers, but of their *ideal representations of themselves*. This means it's not just any murder, but a murder of the ideal figure, the father: a patricide. Through their game pieces, Dee and Dennis identify themselves with movie stars who meet cultural ideals of physical beauty, while Charlie and Mac identify with action figures who meet cultural ideals of toughness and brawn.

Win or lose, all the players get to participate in the destruction of one another's best selves without admitting to themselves what they're doing. And that's what the Gang is all about. The four children collaborate to create a space where they're free from the inner critic that lets the voice of their parents rule their lives: a City of Brotherly Love. Their attempt fails, of course. Freeing oneself from the grip of unrealizable ideals is an unrealizable ideal, and the satisfaction of playing CharDee MacDennis keeps them in denial. Their city's walled, yes, but not windowed; it's run-down, rat-infested, and never, ever sunny in Paddy's Pub.

6
Are the Gang Authentic?

CHARLOTTE KNOWLES

Now I can't be the only one who thinks Night Crawlers sounds like an awesome game—although perhaps writing rules for it and forcing your friends to play it puts me in the minority.

If you say you haven't at least been tempted to play real life Hungry Hungry Hippos with grapes, a table, and a good friend, then you're definitely lying.

And come on, admit it, Kitten Mittens actually does sounds like quite a good idea.

Mac's cut off T-shirts? A strong look! Although Artemis's bleached asshole? Yeah, maybe give that one a miss.

Not only has *It's Always Sunny* brought us these life enhancing ideas—and many more—it also challenges us to think about what constitutes 'normal', everyday ways of life. A philosopher who presents us with a similar task is the twentieth-century German phenomenologist Martin Heidegger.

In his major work, *Being and Time* (1927), Heidegger describes the tendency we have to conform to standard norms and average ways of life. This love of averageness, getting lost in the crowd—doing what "they" do, liking what "they" like, behaving how "they" behave—is for Heidegger the definitive way of life for most people most of the time and, roughly speaking, losing oneself in this averageness and getting carried along by others, constitutes what he calls an 'inauthentic' way of life.

Milk-Steak

'Averageness' and 'normality' seem to be the last words you'd use to describe the Gang's way of life. For the most part they appear to be an independent unit, freed from societal norms of decency and good manners. Not only that, a lot of what Heidegger might call their 'everyday ways of Being' are just freakin' weird. Think about Charlie's set up: feasting on wolf hair and cat food, huffing glue, being stalked by cats, and sharing a bed with a geriatric homunculus. Okay, maybe some of those we could put down to lack of funds, but what about in "The Waitress Is Getting Married" when Dennis and Mac try and make him a dating profile?

> DENNIS: Let's talk about your likes and dislikes. Umm . . . how about your favorite food, what would that be?
>
> CHARLIE: Oh, milk-steak.
>
> DENNIS AND MAC: [*simultaneously*] Hmm?
>
> DENNIS: What?
>
> CHARLIE: Milk-steak.
>
> DENNIS: I'm not putting milk-steak.
>
> MAC: Just put regular steak and then—
>
> CHARLIE: Don't put regular steak, put milk-steak, she'll know what it is.
>
> DENNIS: No she won't know what it is! Nobody knows what that is. Okay, alright what's your favorite hobby?
>
> CHARLIE: Uhh . . . magnets.
>
> DENNIS: Wha— like making magnets, collecting magnets?
>
> MAC: Playing with magnets?
>
> CHARLIE: Just magnets.
>
> DENNIS: I'm just gonna put snowboarding. We'll just put snowboarding.

As we can see, Charlie's tastes are far from 'average' and certainly don't conform to the norm (he goes onto list 'ghouls' as his likes and 'knees' as his dislikes). So if Charlie's way of life can't be described as average, generic and in this respect inauthentic, how can we describe it? For Heidegger, if a way of life is not inauthentic, then it's authentic. This 'authentic' way of life is often caricatured as a kind of radical individualism—breaking away from all societal norms and striking out on your own to live a completely unique existence. We can certainly say Charlie's life is 'unique', but does it really capture what Heidegger means by 'authentic'?

Charlie's dream book ("Charlie Kelly: King of the Rats"), containing such mystical creatures as "denim chicken," "bird with teeth," and "worm hat" (not a hat for a worm, nor a hat made of worms, but a German pilot named Hans Wermhatt), suggest a rather warped mind, and when combined with his strongly held belief that he is an expert in "bird law" ("The Gang Exploits the Mortgage Crisis"), it seems that Charlie is closer to a delusional mad man than some kind of authentic ideal. Indeed, as the lawyer tells him in "The Gang Exploits the Mortgage Crisis": "I can see clearly you know nothing about the law. It seems like you have a tenuous grasp of the English language in general." I think that about sums it up.

Okay, so Charlie's not a contender for an authentic way of life, which means there must be more to authenticity than simply transcending the ordinary, and indeed there is. Heidegger talks about authenticity as a transformation or 'modification' of everyday, inauthentic ways of life. So rather than an authentic way of life being one in which we totally transcend the everyday—freeing ourselves from the shackles of normality—being authentic seems to mean something like finding a different way of relating to everyday ways of life. Whereas the inauthentic person drifts along without ever really taking a stand on their existence, the authentic person endorses the life choices they've made and the social roles they occupy. For example, the Waitress might be said to live an inauthentic life because she just drifts along in her job, she doesn't seem to endorse the choices she's made or the role she occupies. In this respect Charlie might be said to be more authentic than her, he really does seem to enjoy all his "Charlie Work". His set up with Frank seems to be something he's chosen, rather than a way of life he's simply fallen into. In "The Gang Gives Frank an Intervention" we hear Charlie bemoan the fact that he and Frank "aren't really making memories together anymore" and in "Dennis Looks Like a Registered Sex Offender" we see how hurt Charlie is when Frank leaves him to shack up with his "Bang-Maid" (a.k.a. Charlie's Mom). The Waitress, however, appears to hate her job, and her life, she doesn't seem to endorse the choices she's made, even as she's making them. In "Mac's Big Break" we see that she's prepared to drink soup out of Frank's shoe, albeit for the princely sum of $500, but that doesn't seem to be something she's endorsed—a choice she can get behind, a choice which says something about her as an authentic individual—rather it's come about as the result of a situation in which she's simply found herself. She's rolling with the punches, or in this case, with the buckets of dirty dishwater . . .

My Dick through a Wall

FRANK: Charlie, you showed a lot of balls stealing my money. That shows leadership. I'm promoting you to manager.

MAC: What about me Frank? I stole a shitload of your money!

FRANK: You get DICK because you're a follower and a thief.

In "Dennis and Dee go on Welfare" we see Frank condemning Mac for being a "follower," suggesting that, by extension, he also condemns the inauthentic way of life, which has such a tendency towards 'following'—being led, rather than leading. Is Frank, then, a good candidate for authenticity? He certainly seems to be self-directed and actively making choices, rather than simply 'following the crowd'. He's given up his plush yuppie lifestyle and his mansion to live in squalor like he used to ("Charlie Gets Crippled"). He seems unbounded by societal norms of good manners and decency, as is evidenced by his grotesque eating habits—remember the rum ham ("The Gang Goes to the Jersey Shore"), or all those sandwiches, dripping down his chin. Those are the actions of an uninhibited man. Frank continually endorses the choices he's made. He's making the most of his life, as he tells us in "The Gang Gives Frank an Intervention." When questioned about why he would want to bang his sister-in-law at her husband's funeral, he replies: "Well, I don't know how many years on this Earth I got left. I'm going to get really weird with it." And why not? Enjoy it while you can, right?

But even though Frank has little to no regard for social taboos or niceties, in some areas of his life he does seem to follow a 'script'—indeed, quite literally so—rather than carving out his own path. I am thinking, of course, of his allusions to his previous life:

> FRANK: Oh yeah? Well, I was hunted once. I'd just come back from 'Nam. I was hitching through Oregon and some cop started harassing me. Next thing you know, I had a whole army of cops chasing me through the woods! I had to take 'em all out—it was a bloodbath!

> [*everyone pauses awkwardly*]

> CHARLIE: That's Rambo, dude.

> FRANK: What?

> CHARLIE: You just described the plot of *Rambo*.

In "Mac and Dennis: Man Hunters" we see Frank relying quite explicitly on what the Heideggerean scholar Nancy J. Holland might call a 'cultural script' in order to understand himself. Namely the script from the first *Rambo* movie. But for Holland, the idea that we rely on scripts to understand ourselves and help us live our lives need not be taken this literally. Scripts are practices, behaviors, and social roles that are not unique to us as individuals. For example, 'alcoholic', 'mother' and 'teacher' could all be considered scripts. They are shared ways of life that can be taken up and 'performed' by anyone. The notion of a 'script' seems to capture something about the inauthentic way of life, as it suggests following a course that has already been mapped out for us, implying that our actions are not fully of our own choosing. 'Rambo' isn't perhaps a typical script, although it is certainly a way of life that Frank has taken up (or at least imagined he's taken up) from another source. Nevertheless, as we see with Frank, he doesn't realize he's living out a script, protesting that it's truly *his own unique life* that he's describing. And indeed, inauthentic people may not realize they're being inauthentic or conforming to cultural scripts instead of making their own decisions about how to live their lives. However, that is not to say that a script couldn't be lived out consciously. We see such an example in Dee's emulation of *Sex and the City* ("Who Pooped the Bed?").

Blast My Nips

In "Who Pooped the Bed?" Dee attempts to "play *Sex and the City*"—as Dennis puts it—recruiting Artemis and The Waitress to be in her new girly gang. They go to a Martini bar that's just opened. Dee wants them to drink cosmopolitans, talk about men, and generally emulate the 'classy' ladies of *Sex and the City*. They each have a role to perform: Artemis is "the sassy one who always plays by her own rules"; The Waitress is . . . an alcoholic. Oh. And with this revelation, shortly followed by Artemis's announcement that she has a "bleached asshole" (in her defense, "he was going to find out anyway"), things start to go downhill. Rather than being the classy group of girlfriends Dee imagines, they're a rag-tag bunch of sexually desperate, violent drunks, with apparently massive feet.

Whereas Frank confuses his life with that of John Rambo, Dee conforms to a far more 'normal' social narrative, albeit in a bizarre way. Even when all the odds are against her, Dee still attempts to perform the *Sex and the City* script: trying to squeeze her size thirteen canal barges into the $700 Manolo Blahniks she can't afford, whilst the owner of the shop advises her she might be better off in the "Big 'n' Tall store" down the street. In her attempt to adopt the classy life style she's seen on the silver screen, Dee can be said to live an inauthentic life. Although we've argued that authenticity need not involve transcending the everyday, it nevertheless involves a certain kind of—potentially critical—relation to everyday ways of life. The kind of relation where we recognize the culturally intelligible possibilities and social roles that are open to us—acknowledging that these are necessarily shared and thus in this sense inauthentic—and yet we nevertheless attempt to occupy these roles and live out these possibilities in our own unique ways. Rather than simply aping these ways of life unquestioningly. Dee doesn't seem to make her own choices, or carve out her own individual way of being a 'classy individual'. Nor does she realize that such a way of life is not really open to her, given the facts of her situation. Instead she allows her behavior to be dictated by the cultural narrative she's adopted. Dee's behavior shows us that the more obediently we perform scripts, the less we are unique, self-directed individuals, and thus the less we can be considered authentic.

Makeup

We might say, then, that Dee's life, at least in "Who Pooped the Bed?" is governed by cultural norms of what it is to be a successful woman. These manifest in very practical terms: drinking cosmopolitans, wearing Manolo Blahniks, (supposedly) eating at fancy restaurants. These are all material signifiers of wealth and success, and show that she is living in accordance with a certain cultural 'script'. But the signals of an inauthentic life do not have to be this concrete. As we have seen, scripts are fairly specific, 'filled out' ways of life—the New York socialite, the housewife, the drug addict—they roughly determine how we will act in a given situation, if we are to faithfully follow the script. However, there are broader social and cultural norms, with more fuzzy boundaries, which also make up the content of everyday life, a strong adherence to which might be seen to constitute an inauthentic way of life. Dennis is perhaps the best example of this form of inauthenticity.

In "The Aluminium Monster vs. Fatty Magoo" we see Dennis's obsession with dominant Western standards of beauty. 'Obsession' is certainly the right word, as we see him dismiss models—criticizing them for their small boobs, or their big waists—until he identifies himself as the only one truly capable of showing off the dresses to their full potential. Dennis's mind is clearly warped, but in a different way to Charlie's. Whereas Charlie's dreams and aspirations seem to have no clear basis in cultural norms, or indeed reality, Dennis's are firmly rooted in what is deemed to be culturally acceptable and desirable. He continually 'pops off' his shirt to reveal his well-toned body and "always wear[s] a little bit of make-up" ("The Gang Gets Stranded in the Woods"). However, Dennis takes these cultural norms and expectations to the extreme. In "The High School Reunion Part 2: The Gang's Revenge" we see this exchange:

> **CHRISTIE:** Dude, you're wearing makeup.
>
> **DENNIS:** Yeah, I'm wearing a little bit of makeup. Who doesn't . . . ?
>
> **CHRISTIE:** And a girdle.
>
> **DENNIS:** Yeah, I wanted to seem thin for the occasion. That's not weird.

It's definitely weird. Dennis seems to go through inauthenticity and come out the other side. He certainly occupies the cultural norms of beauty in his own unique way, but does this make him authentic? I would say not. Dennis is a vain ego-maniac, and potentially a rapist ("The Gang Buys a Boat", "The High School Reunion Part 2: The Gang's Revenge," "The Aluminum Monster vs. Fatty Magoo." I could go on . . .). Although Dennis takes up cultural norms in his own unique way, he seems completely dominated by them. In "Dennis Looks Like a Registered Sex Offender" he's more bothered by the fact the gang say he looks like a fat man, than the fact that that fat man is a registered sex offender. Similarly, in "The Gang Gets Successful," Dennis undergoes a chemical peel in order to live up to the expectation of "physical perfection" he thinks the others have of him, but instead ends up looking like he's wearing a mask of himself over his own face. Ultimately, then, Dennis seems to be ruled by the norm of beauty, rather than occupying it in unique way.

Pro-Choice Is Pro-Death

So none of the rest of the gang truly live up to the high ideals of authenticity. Even if they lead lives completely out of the ordinary (Charlie), endorse the choices they've made (Frank), live out culturally recognizable scripts (Dee), or enact social norms in their own unique way (Dennis), they also seem to have aspects of their lives that are profoundly inauthentic.

Which leaves us with Mac. Mac might seem like a strong contender for authenticity. He doesn't have a completely bizarre way of life, but at the same time he stands by the choices he's made and the ways of life he values. Unfortunately, these are cut-off T-shirts, religious zealotry and homophobia—possibly rooted in a latent homosexuality ("Mac Day"). Moreover, once he's committed to something, Mac sees it through to the end ("How Mac Got Fat"). However, he does seem very susceptible to peer-pressure and clearly cares about how others view him. For example, he's afraid to tell the gang that he's banging Carman, the pre-op transsexual ("Mac Is a Serial Killer"), despite the fact they seem to have a genuine connection, as is evidenced by his reaction to her subsequent marriage ("Mac Fights Gay Marriage"). In a sense, then, Mac is very driven by conforming to norms, and not doing anything out of the ordinary. Indeed, as Frank says, he is a "follower" ("Dennis and Dee Go on Welfare"), and he often seems eager to please.

In fact, Mac is the most conservative of the gang. As noted above, he is highly religious, disapproves of homosexuality ("Mac Fights Gay Marriage") and abortion ("Charlie wants an Abortion") and is obsessed with packing on body mass ("Mac and Dennis Break Up"). Unlike Dennis who thinks it's perfectly normal for a man to wear make-up and a girdle, Mac is immured in cultural norms of masculinity: forever 'getting his pump on', wanting to show off his tattoos, and generally boasting about how badass he is—even providing the Gang with documentary evidence ("Mac's Banging the Waitress"). However, in "Mac Day" we see the making of one of these Project Badass videos. Mac tells the gang it would be far too dangerous to *actually* jump off the bridge, so instead they'll just make it look like he did. But before he has time to set up the shoot, Country Mac goes right ahead and jumps, emerging from the water beer still in hand. Now that's badass.

Putting on Airs?

All the members of the Gang exhibit some authentic traits and some inauthentic ones. This is actually very fitting, since for Heidegger, authenticity and inauthenticity don't seem to be mutually exclusive—a question of either/or—rather, the question of 'authentic or inauthentic?' seems to be answered by 'necessarily both'. Authenticity and inauthenticity are matters of degree. At times—like when we're trying to live like the girls from *Sex and the City*—we might be said to be more inauthentic; and at others—like when we're eating rum ham on the beach—we might be said to be more authentic. If inauthenticity is necessarily associated with everyday shared ways of life, then we can never totally escape it. Even though Charlie might have an 'unconventional' lifestyle he nevertheless occupies shared possibilities—getting boozed, working in a pub, pursuing women; well, one woman. Moreover, Heidegger stresses that authenticity and inauthenticity are not value judgments, nor are they moral concepts. So Dennis could be an authentic rapist and maybe Frank's desire to bang his sister-in-law at the funeral of her husband is an authentic desire. The authentic-inauthentic distinction, then, is more about how we relate to cultural norms and the way in which we occupy social roles. Although at first it may seem that the gang's rejection of social norms of decency and human kindness mark them out as authentic individuals, when you scratch beneath the surface, much of their way of life is structured by cultural norms and societal expectations, thus showing that they're not necessarily any more authentic than the rest of us, bitches.

III

Virtue

7
The Gang's Quest for Happiness—One Day at a Time

KYLE ALKEMA AND ADAM BARKMAN

If the members of the Gang were to choose a theme song for themselves, our best guess is—if they could agree on one—that it would be Sheryl Crow's 1996 hit "If It Makes You Happy."

"If it makes you happy / it can't be that bad" she belts out, and it doesn't take much imagination to hear the Gang singing along with her. Drinking 'til they're thirsty again sums them up pretty well: they are self-proclaimed drunks who own a bar.

If It Makes You Happy . . .

From the first episode we see that the four members of the Gang in *It's Always Sunny in Philadelphia*—Mac, Charlie, Dennis, and Dennis's twin sister Deandra, or Sweet Dee—will do whatever they think has a chance at making them happy. The problem, though, is with the word "happy." What would it take for each one of the Gang to be truly happy? Happy by their standards might turn out to be very different than what a contemplative philosopher might say. A whole lot hinges on whether happiness is, or should be, something that we can all agree on, or if it is something that we are all left to figure out for ourselves.

Mac, Charlie, and Dennis are three friends in their late twenties who are bonded together by Paddy's Pub, the Irish

79

bar they co-own, with Sweet Dee as their bartender. Paddy's Pub is not run very well and seems to be more of an opportunity for the Gang to keep partying, rather than being a serious business venture or a career choice: in their words, "it's who we are" and "all we've got," and so they can "get laid."

Once we become emotionally bonded to the Gang, we want them to be successful, healthy, and, above all, happy: that should be our proper response. It's tough to watch them do harm to others, but it's much tougher to watch them do harm to themselves—they repeatedly shoot themselves in the foot, and one even literally shoots another in the head.

Happiness, for them, is whatever brings pleasure and makes them feel good, usually in the short-term. They are free to pursue instant gratification without worrying about the consequences. If it makes them happy, then it can't be that bad, right? Is this how we should approach happiness?

. . . Then It Can't Be That Bad

A long time ago—over two thousand years—in a country far, far away—Greece—a man thought about what makes for a good life. His name was Aristotle and he came up with a theory to explain how we can get the most out of life. He agreed to some extent with the Gang—he thought that our main concern should be with our own wellbeing and that we should seek pleasure. But then, his thoughts took a different turn.

Aristotle claimed that we don't always act in our own best interests if we impulsively grab at everything which looks tasty. Instead, we would do better to train ourselves to follow certain broad principles called virtues. These principles enable us to get the most satisfaction out of life in the long run.

One of Aristotle's famous ideas is that of the Golden Mean. The best way to act is a middle way between two extremes. For example, never being willing to stand up for yourself would be *cowardice*, while always being eager to aggressively assert your interests would be *recklessness*. The golden mean between these two extremes would be *courage*.

According to Aristotle, the choices we make will be influenced by the habits we have adopted, and if we develop virtuous habits, we will tend to make good choices, and this will maximize our happiness in the long run.

We sometimes see the Gang groping for some kind of Aristotelian principle of virtue. For example, Mac nearly practices the virtue of wisdom when he says, "We're not going to get anywhere yelling at each other, alright? We need to be rational," but his conclusion lets him down: "I think it's clear what needs to happen: we need to buy a gun" ("Gun Fever").

Aristotle's approach has been called a Virtue Ethic. Its opposite might be called a Reverse Virtue Ethic. For instance, instead of practicing virtue by choosing the mean between two extremes, a Reverse Virtue Ethic would always try the extremes first. This would be a crude method of trial and error: do what works, and if something doesn't work then don't do it again. If at first you don't succeed, try something else.

Sniffing—really sniffing—gasoline to see if it is, indeed, gasoline, and then sniffing some more is an example of exploring one end of the spectrum, rather than, say, using deduction, reading the label, or gently wafting the fumes carefully ("Flowers for Charlie").

Since Charlie, Mac, Dennis, and Sweet Dee definitely do not shy away from exploring potentially immoral or harmful situations, the odds seem favorable that they follow a type of Reverse Virtue Ethic; however, their understanding of the Good and what it means to them is unclear. Happiness, for the Gang, is merely pleasurable feeling, and for them the Good refers to *anything* that will lead to those feelings.

There are three major roads that the members of the Gang travel in their attempts to find pleasure: first, the road to acquiring stuff; second, the road to fulfilling lust; and third, the road to receiving validation.

For Their Own Benefit

The first road the Gang often travels is one they hope is like a rainbow with a pot of unguarded gold at the end of it. Each member of the Gang is selfish; their desire for an instant payoff clouds their judgment, but their efforts consistently fail to pay off. Getting money quickly and easily makes them feel good, as does spending it. The problem for them is that things always spiral out of control to the harm of all involved throughout the series.

The Gang puts their lazy greed before the well-being of others in an effort to experience maximal pleasure. They'll try just about *anything* if it means making a quick buck. They serve teenagers watered-down alcohol until things start to get out of hand, which for the Gang means being sucked into high school drama and having their feelings hurt ("Underage Drinking: A National Concern"). When Paddy's Pub is turned into a gay bar by a newly hired promoter, the Gang is seduced by the huge increase in business and go along with it at first, but stop after things go too far: Sweet Dee and Mac get Dennis hammered on tequila and Dennis wakes up the next morning in bed with two naked men ("The Gang Gets Racist").

In the second season, Dennis and Sweet Dee's dad—Frank Reynolds, the man who raised them but is not their real father—comes back into their lives, wanting to give his money to poor people and spend more time with the two of them. Dennis and Sweet Dee don't care about spending time with him; they only care about the money, so they rob their own parents' house ("Charlie Gets Crippled"). In "A Very Sunny Christmas" Frank sums them up pretty well: "You don't give a shit whether I change or not, do you? Huh? It's all about you, what you want, gimme gimme gimme . . ."

Even when they seem to want to do some good for others, they still manage to make it about themselves, as Mac demonstrates when he says, "Wait a second, maybe helping other people is the best way to help ourselves" ("The Gang Gets Extreme: Home Makeover Edition"). Predictably, no one is better off by the end of that episode.

The members of the Gang do more damage to themselves than they do to others (although this point could be argued: they really do some serious damage all around). In "Dennis and Dee Go on Welfare," Dennis is all gung-ho about following his dreams and achieving his goals, until he qualifies for unemployment insurance—which pays more than he was making at Paddy's—but to qualify for welfare Dennis and Sweet Dee claim to be recovering crack addicts. Unfortunately, they have to get it verified with blood work, so they try to have just enough crack cocaine to pass the blood test, and promptly get addicted.

Another time, the Gang runs for office with the intention of soliciting a bribe to drop out of the race, and things get out of control: Charlie loses his Garbage Pail Babies card collection, Mac has his life 'threatened' and is intimidated by cops in on the prank ("The Gang Runs for Office"). In "The Gang Sells Out," they agree to sell the bar for a quick payday, planning for a life of leisure and retirement (kicking Sweet Dee to the curb because she's not a shareholder), but Frank tries to milk it for all it's worth. Of course the plan backfires and things go horribly wrong. Amazingly, at one point Dennis and Charlie ditch Mac, Sweet Dee, and Frank in a forest, and waste ten thousand dollars taking a jet eighty miles to a casino in Atlantic City ("The Gang Gets Stranded in the Woods"). Most of their efforts are self-destructive.

The Gang often does not hesitate in pursuing something that may benefit them and satisfy their greed; their Reverse Virtue Ethic ensures this. When Dennis seems to attempt a change of heart, saying, "I can do good. I am capable of doing good," Mac puts him in his place: "No, you just screw people over for your own benefit" ("The Gang Finds a Dumpster Baby"). Whatever feels good is good.

For a Chance to Get Laid

The second road the Gang travels is one going nowhere in particular, littered with sexual dalliances along the way—and the more, the better. Happiness in this case comes through instant gratification: there is no place for healthy or long-term emotional relationships of any kind.

The Gang will try pretty much *anything* if it might result in "erotic conquests" (in Dennis's sophisticated words). Mac joins the anti-abortion movement to hook up with one of the protestors; Dennis is going to join Mac until he concludes that the pro-choice side might have more available targets ("Charlie Wants an Abortion"). In the episode "Charlie Has Cancer," Charlie tells Dennis that he has cancer, trying for a shot at the Waitress (hoping Dennis will set her up with him out of pity), and then Dennis and Mac use the line to get sympathy from women. After Charlie is run over by Dennis in his SUV, Mac, Dennis, and Sweet Dee pretend to be crippled to gain sympathy (or pity) for a chance at a fling; Charlie is the one in a wheelchair with two broken legs, but even he has to take it further by pretending to be a war veteran ("Charlie Gets Crippled"). This is obviously not sustainable behavior, only a feeble attempt at temporary satisfaction.

Nothing exemplifies this temporality better than the episode about Dennis's strategy for making women fall in love with him just so he can sleep with them a few times, before stopping communication completely (which is the "S" in the D.E.N.N.I.S. System). As Dennis puts it so eloquently, his system is "a comprehensive approach to seduction that I have perfected over the years. See, my success with women does not solely stem from my good looks and my charm; there is a careful, systemic approach that has allowed me to become the playboy that I am today" ("The D.E.N.N.I.S. System"). Dates are a waste of time and money to Dennis. As Dennis is lecturing about his elaborate system, Sweet Dee accuses Dennis of being a sociopath and Dennis doesn't disagree. Then Mac follows with his M.A.C. system (Move in After Completion), who is fittingly followed by Frank (with his magnum condoms and his stack of hundreds).

The Gang pushes the boundaries in their attempts to satisfy their lust. Again, their Reverse Virtue Ethic manifests itself pragmatically. When Sweet Dee's conscience chimes in, "Are you actually going to throw away all of your convictions for a chance to get laid?" Dennis simply replies, "I don't really have any convictions," which probably, in his defense, isn't strictly true ("Charlie Wants an Abortion").

They're Just Really, Really Vain

The third road the Gang travels is one they hope is lined with rows of people on either side seeing them for how awesome they truly are, with a trophy at the end of it. They pose as being assured of their superiority, but they are constantly seeking validation from other people, especially from the others in the Gang.

Dennis, Mac, Sweet Dee, and even Charlie will all go to great lengths for external validation. Dennis is by far the vainest of the four. He is obsessed with his looks (and intelligence and success and athleticism), and needs everyone to know just how amazing he is. Mac and Dennis compete over the attentions of the granddaughter of an old man who died in their bar ("The Gang Finds a Dead Guy"). At one point Dennis declares, "I will always win in these circumstances," and it quickly degenerates into childish bickering (although, to be fair, Dennis does come out on top).

In the disturbing episode "Charlie Got Molested," Mac tries to validate his attractiveness by making himself available to his former high school phys. ed. teacher (a falsely accused child molester). Mac is allured by a transvestite when she compliments his body—"you're ripped," she says—after he finds out she has a certain male reproductive organ ("Charlie Has Cancer"). All of them warp their memory of high school so that they can think of themselves as popular, and then Mac and Charlie are persuaded to buy alcohol for the high school party by being told how cool they are and how cool they would be if they bought the keg—"it would be the coolest thing ever" ("Underage Drinking: A National Concern"). Their happiness seems to be dependent on validation from the world, and it doesn't matter how this is achieved.

The Gang also embraces a get-even policy of revenge throughout the series. For example, when Mac sees Charlie destroying a tape (that he thinks is his one from Mac's Project Badass collection), Mac tries to sleep with the Waitress, who Charlie is in love with, out of revenge ("Mac's Banging the Waitress"). The whole episode descends into competition and payback, and it gets very messy. Dennis and Mac compete to pick up women in the mall in their wheelchairs, and it ends with the only way to settle a competition like able-bodied gentlemen: by wheelchair racing. The scene ends with the two of them fighting each other, out of their wheelchairs, in the middle of the mall. In the same episode, Charlie and Frank start fighting, and Frank and Sweet Dee fight as well; by the end of it, it is summed up nicely when Mac says, "We are so lucky that nobody got killed" ("Charlie Gets Crippled"). In one ridiculous episode, Charlie tries to get even with Dennis for threatening to sleep with the Waitress by encouraging Mac to sleep with Dennis's mom and then bringing Dennis by the house in time to see Mac leaving, so Dennis tries to seduce Mac's mom out of revenge—and that's only part of the episode. It's all fueled by the desire to be crowned the champion.

Much of the Gang's self-esteem and self-worth is determined by how they perceive what others think about them. In the episode where Paddy's Pub is temporarily turned into a gay bar, Dennis likes the attention from the gay men, and he doesn't think about potential consequences when he plays up to it and encourages their attentions. When he tries to defend his flirting, Sweet Dee hits back: "You're not gay, you're just really, really vain" ("The Gang Gets Racist"). In this case the consequence is that when he wakes up the next morning there is a naked man in his bed and another naked man that comes into his room and slaps Dennis's rear end: lesson learned.

For Once in Our Lives

The road the Gang travels is not lined with good intentions, but maybe there are some good intentions scattered along the way: the members of the Gang have their limits. Their limits are determined by their consciences. Much of their banter is arguing about the rightness or wrongness of something, or trying to justify something they all know is wrong. Mac tries to justify selling (watered down) alcohol to minors by talking about their social responsibility and that they might "actually be doing something good"; then Charlie contradicts this when his defense is that "this isn't a morality contest" ("Underage Drinking: A National Concern").

They do have standards and limits: in the same episode Dennis, to his credit, says no to the high school student coming on to him, at least until she blackmails him to take her to the prom (to make her ex-boyfriend jealous). Mac and Charlie draw the line at selling Nazi paraphernalia to a museum, rather than on eBay, which would be "like, illegal, or . . . maybe a little immoral" ("The Gang Finds a Dead Guy"). At different points in the series they try to "really do some good in Philadelphia," but again mostly operate from selfish motives (for example in "The Gang Runs for Office").

The ethics of decision-making—the rightness or wrongness of a situation—comes up time and again throughout the series. The Gang critiques themselves, each other, and are critiqued by those around them. Dennis, in a misguided effort (of course), shows this when he says, "let's do the right thing for once in our lives" ("How Mac Got Fat").

Pushing Their Luck with the Big Guy Upstairs

What sets their limits—and guides their consciences—seems to be their roots in Catholicism. Sweet Dee goes to confession where she confesses that she hasn't been in ten years, yet she still wears a cross ("The Gang Exploits a Miracle"). Mac repeatedly invokes God's wrath—"God will smite you all"— as well as the doom of Hell—"Let him die and burn in Hell"—on those who cross his path ("The Gang Exploits a Miracle," "Charlie Got Molested," and "Gun Fever"). Mac goes to confession regularly; at confession he once asks that God smite his friends because he blames them for making him fat ("How Mac Got Fat"). Mac and Charlie defend abortion from a Catholic perspective (and condemn birth control), but are criticized by Sweet Dee for regularly having premarital sex, to which they don't have a defense ("Charlie Wants an Abortion").

In "The Gang Finds a Dumpster Baby," Dennis seems to have a change of heart when he wants to do some good and make a difference, but he is scoffed at by Mac and Sweet Dee, although Dennis seems to care more about what the world will say about him after he dies. They have some belief in God and Hell, but seem resigned to their own damnation: Mac is worried about "pushing our luck with the Big Guy upstairs on this one," to which Charlie replies, "Dude, if you don't think you're already going to Hell, you need to take a long look at yourself" ("The Gang Exploits a Miracle"). If they didn't believe in God in some sense, at least, then it is tough to see why much of their talk is about Him.

Catholicism has usually embraced the Aristotelian Virtue Ethic in some form, while adding the Christian virtues of faith, hope, and love. Since each member of the Gang exhibits some kind of Catholic influence, an Aristotelian Virtue Ethic critique of the Gang is warranted. The Aristotelian Virtue Ethic aims for developing a virtuous character by meditating on what the best and right course of action should be and then acting on it. There are hints throughout the series that the Gang approaches this ethic: efforts are possibly made at virtuous growth. One example is Mac's idea of a 'tipping point'. The idea is that if they keep doing the right thing it will eventually pay off. But, then again, Mac calls being "psychotically vain, or needy and pathetic, or just plain sad" the right things to be to reach this point ("How Mac Got Fat").

The Gang has an undefined and perverted sense of the consequences for doing the wrong thing. When Sweet Dee criticizes Dennis and Mac for their seemingly unethical behavior, Mac can only reply, "Look at Sweet Dee, sitting on her cloud of judgment, handing down life lessons to all the sinners" ("Charlie Gets Crippled").

One Day at a Time

Where does that leave us with virtue ethics and happiness? The Gang is clearly confused by the notion of right and wrong: their arguing and attempts to justify immoral actions reveals this. They are also confused about happiness: they have no concept of long-term happiness or flourishing, but rather remain trapped in the present and the short-term of 'whatever feels good must be good'. When Sweet Dee remarks, "I don't know how you guys live with yourselves," their only reply is "one day at a time," even though she's no better than Dennis, Mac, or Charlie ("Underage Drinking: A National Concern").

Unfortunately for the Gang, they are philosophically and ethically lazy because they have not thought through morality. If they had a robust understanding of either an Aristotelian Virtue Ethic or a Reverse Virtue Ethic their consciences might be much cleaner and they could focus on pursuing happiness, whether that happiness is virtuous flourishing or instant gratification.

We can't forget that this is a TV show: things go out of control because they are meant to. We might want the Gang to be happy—and we might even want the Gang to do what we would think is the right thing—but the members of the Gang are the way they are because that's what works for the show. It wouldn't have lasted into its tenth season otherwise.

But, unfortunately for them, the Gang offers to show us the path not to take; fortunately, they are fictional characters. Maybe they are reverse role models: maybe they experience the evil ends of the spectrum so that we don't have to. Who knows, it might be the point of the show. Maybe we should thank them.

8
Frank Reynolds, Role Model

ADAM HENSCHKE

The world of *It's Always Sunny* is populated with horrible people—each more morally bankrupt than the last. Frank Reynolds may be a moral sinkhole, given that he is the cause of many moral failings of the Gang: In "Dennis and Dee's Mom Is Dead" Bruce Mathis lays the blame for Dennis and Deandra's moral failings at Frank's feet. Frank seems to be a moral monster, without redeeming qualities. Yet in one fundamental sense Frank is not only virtuous, but may surprisingly be a role model.

The other four members of the Gang are all suffering from self-delusions.

- **Charlie: endless pursuit of the Waitress**
- **Dee: dreams of success as a comedienne/actress**
- **Mac: his extreme masculinity**
- **Dennis: the Golden God**

It's true that a certain level of self-delusion is needed for self-creation, growth, and change. Yet too much self-delusion makes sure that a person will never achieve their goals. As we see, the Gang's dreams always fail. Compare the Gang to Matthew 'Rickety Cricket' Mara, who instead loses hope for change. The important point is that a person should chart a balanced or 'virtuous course' when working on reality and character.

Frank is an example of virtue here—he rejected the delusions of his marriage, but still indulges in willful acts of self-creation. Frank recognizes that reality is important but needs balance with self-creation. And if we look closer, we get to the unlikely conclusion: Frank not only has some virtue, but is actually something of a role model!

Throwing Stones

Seeing the corruption of other's character is fascinating: We like to witness things we would never do; maybe to judge others, maybe to feel better about ourselves, maybe to vicariously experience something taboo. *It's Always Sunny* presents a veritable festival of moral monsters to choose from. Whether it's the bizarre sexual practices of Artemis, the incestuous clan McPoyle, or the sheer offensiveness of Gayle the Snail, this is a really horrible community of people.

However, these characters are a side-stage to the main show that is the Gang. Individually and collectively they keep dragging us back in part to see how much lower they can sink. As semi-patriarchal figurehead of the Gang, Frank Reynolds stands out as a ringmaster of moral ruination. It's safe to say that calling Frank an 'exemplar of virtue' is unexpected—shocking even. Yet we can all learn something from Frank! Our own moral character could be improved if we took a leaf from his book.

Exemplars of Virtue

In the ancient past, character development was seen as important, perhaps the *fundamental* question of morality. Instead of asking questions like 'What should I *do*?', Greek thinkers like Aristotle were more interested in the question of 'What sort of person should I *be*?'

In his *Nicomachean Ethics*, written 2,500 years ago, Aristotle wrote that virtue is concerned with practical wisdom.

The virtuous choice is finding the mean between two extremes—not too much and not too little. So the virtuous choice is found in between two vices. For instance, someone who hangs on desperately to every penny he has is an example of the vice of greed, while someone who gives all he possesses away to panhandlers is being irresponsibly wasteful and improvident. Both extremes are vices, whereas someone who looks after himself but also spares something to help out others would be an example of the virtue of generosity.

A person with practical wisdom will be someone with a lot of life experience. So, Aristotle claims that younger and less experienced people should look to more experienced people. If they think of Frank as a person who has lived a lot and has therefore accumulated mucho practical wisdom, they might ask themselves 'What would Frank do?' and model their actions on his.

Self-Delusion

The Gang present us with a great set of characters to learn from: they tell us what *not* to do. They give us master classes in how to ruin lives, whether it's their own or those around them. While each member of the Gang has a range of deep personal flaws, they all share something: the vice of self-delusion. Specifically, this is a *vice* where *the desire to self-create has become unbalanced*. It means that the Gang will never achieve what they want, and this failure is a failure of practical wisdom. The reason that they are guaranteed to fail is because each member of the Gang has lost contact with reality: *each suffers from an excess of self-delusion*.

We'll start with Charlie and his love for the Waitress. For Charlie, this is an all-consuming love, something that drives many of his actions. This defining point of his character is the desire to love and be loved and is utterly central to who Charlie is. In "The Waitress Is Getting Married," the Gang find out that she's engaged to someone else, and are extremely worried about the possibility that this knowledge will crush Charlie. Mac thinks Charlie may blow his brains out, and Dennis thinks that Charlie "might go postal if he finds about this and kill all of us."

The Waitress knows that Charlie loves her, and continually tells him that she will never date him. Whether it's telling him that she's only acting as his AA sponsor and that she'll never go out on a date with him, that a night spent on the Jersey Shore with him meant she'd "lived out one of her actual nightmares," or rejecting his 'marriage proposal by way of musical' in "The Nightman Cometh," her position is crystal clear:

> THE WAITRESS: Charlie, will I marry you? No, no, I will not. I will never marry you. . . . And I also held up my end of the bargain, so I never have to see you again.
>
> CHARLIE: Okay, so wait. I'm sorry, I want to get this clear. You are saying no?
>
> THE WAITRESS: Oh, I am definitely, definitely saying no.

It's clear as day that she does not love him. Spending time with him is a nightmare. But Charlie can't see this.

So, what's the problem with this? Surely a person needs to have hope in something? Basically, Charlie's blindness to the fact that the Waitress doesn't love him causes problems for him and is dangerous to others. If we think that the general goal of Charlie's pursuit of the Waitress is to love and be loved in return, being so focused on her makes him blind to other women. When "Charlie and Dee Find Love," Ruby Taft, an attractive, nice and very rich woman offers herself to Charlie, but he turns Ruby down. Having the Waitress as his sole pursuit is a failure of practical wisdom: it guarantees that Charlie will never love, will never be loved.

And, earlier in this episode, the Waitress herself implores Charlie to leave her alone, for her sake: "Do you want me to be happy? Yes! Then stop being around every time I turn around! You have to leave me alone!" And, as we saw, if she moved on, it may result in Charlie killing others or himself.

Charlie's delusion that the Waitress will fall in love with him is bad for him, for her, and for the Gang.

Dee-lusion

What of the others? Dee is similar to Charlie; her self-delusion manifests in how she wants others to treat her. Instead of needing love, though, Dee just wants people to like her. Basically, she's after their respect. We see this in her constant delusion of becoming a successful actress/comedienne. When "The Gang Saves the Day," Dee's fantasy world is played out: "the remarkable story of Dee Reynolds, a government witness whose turn as a British butler was so convincing that it was spun off into the highest rated sitcom of all time."

Becoming popular, Dee dreams that she'll become happy and fulfilled, marrying a famous crooner like Josh Groban. She dreams that acting will make this happen. The delusion is not simply that she'll become popular, but this popularity will complete her and make her fulfilled as a person. But she is mostly unwilling to actually work for it. Despite acting being her dream, her way out, she can't be bothered to stick at it. Dennis calls her out on this, calling her a quitter ("Charlie Goes America All Over Everybody's Ass"), to which she responds: "I did try. It just didn't happen to work out."

This is a major problem for Dee. Firstly, when she and Charlie decide to walk a mile in each other's shoes in "Dennis Reynolds: An Erotic Life," we see that she will typically vomit on stage. She knows she isn't good. Much like Charlie, when reality creeps in, she falls into a deep depression. When "The Gang Broke Dee," we see her at her lowest ebb: "The joke's always on me, all right? I get it." But Dennis knows she can get worse and that this will end badly: "Why can't you see that this is the same pattern that you always fall into? Some guy uses you or you use him. And then you know what happens? It's use, use, use, fail, fail, fail, and then it's suicide." Should reality press too hard, she'll end up killing herself.

As for harm to others, given years of abuse and neglect by her family and friends, Dee is largely powerless to harm the Gang. But her unremitting unhappiness means that she will always try to drag down those around her. "I do like to stick it in Dennis's face." Outside of Gang members, she picks on Fatty MaGoo, destroys Rickety Criket's life (more on him later). She'll do whatever she can to make herself feel good, not caring whose life she destroys in the process. Until she's free from the deluded fantasy that she'll become a success through acting/comedy, she won't change.

Mac Attack

Turning to Mac, consider his belief that he is a figure of masculinity. This manifests itself in various ways: his repulsion at Carmen's 'gay' marriage, his command that that the Gang oil up bodybuilding contestants during "Mac Day," his repressed bisexuality. He believes he is a 'Swayze-like' level-headed bouncer, but instead, due to the many stabbings, Paddy's Bar is labelled "The Worst Bar in Philadelphia." What starts off as an attempt to round-house kick his way into a locked car, delusions of his physical attributes grow to think that he can back-flip his way out of an empty pool, or that he is some high-level risk taker in his 'Project-Bad-dass' movies.

The self-delusion reaches its most absurd turn when Mac, in an effort to 'tack on mass' becomes dangerously obese. His self-perception is so distorted that despite being objectively out of shape he believes he's a muscle-bound freak. We learn in "How Mac Got Fat" that he was inspired by a "gorgeous muscle monster" to put on some "serious bulk." In his world, he "went from a tiny twink to the muscle-bound freak you see before you." Yet nothing is further from the truth. This Mac, though large is certainly not a muscle-bound freak: his self-image doesn't even approach reality: self-delusion rules again.

This is a problem for Mac and others. Mac's weight gain is detrimental to his health. In "Frank's Pretty Woman" Dennis and Mac visit a doctor, who tells Mac that he has type-two "diabitis." If Mac's self-perception remains disconnected from reality, he may die prematurely. But as a liberty-loving American, perhaps this unhealthy disconnection from reality is Mac's right?

However, the desire to be ultra-masculine puts others at risk. Throughout the show, Mac fancies himself as an adept bouncer, developing his "ocular pat-down skills." Yet when "The Gang Hits the Road," despite Mac's threat assessment, they pick up a hitchhiker who steals Dee's car. Not only is Mac unable to recognize threats, he's unable to stop them when they occur: In "Hundred Dollar Baby," Mac joins an underground fight-club but is beaten by 'the scrawniest' guy there. Finally, perhaps showing some unconscious awareness of his lack of skills, Mac is a coward. In "Hundred Dollar Baby" he runs away from a mugger threating his friends. Twice. And after joining a citizen's vigilante group to stop "Bums Making a Mess All Over the City," at the first sign of danger he's terrified and tries to escape. Once more, a Gang member's vice of self-delusion puts them and those around them at risk.

The D Man

We complete this list with Dennis, whose self-delusion makes him the most dangerous of the Gang. His self-delusion is that he is wonderful, a perfect creation, "The Golden God." At "The High School Reunion", we see a glimpse of how he sees himself—"I am the king of the mountaintop! I reign supreme over everyone in this school. I am The Golden God of this place. I reign supreme. I! I!" Yet, later in the episode, this status as The Golden God is exposed as a delusion: "Seriously, man, you would just come around saying weird shit about being a golden god or some other insane crap. And referring to all of us as your minions."

The cost to Dennis is seen in his declining physical health and his lack of emotions. In "Frank's Pretty Woman," visiting the doctor with Mac, he confides that his life is "miserable, but it has to be, man. No pain, no gain. I am also constantly in motion. . . . And although I seem relaxed, I'm actually incredibly tense at all times." The medical tests say that

Dennis's lifestyle produces severe dehydration, multiple vitamin deficiencies, anemia, and low blood pressure. Worse still, in later seasons he confesses that he no longer has feelings: "You remember feelings, right?" (Mac Fights Gay Marriage). In creating this idealized self, Dennis is harming his health and undermining the capacity for any meaningful relation with other humans.

Dennis's delusion puts others at risk too. We see his willingness to manipulate people, outlined in a series of steps in "The D.E.N.N.I.S. System." In "The High School Reunion" double episode, we see him attempt to use The D.E.N.N.I.S. System for revenge, trying to sleep with Tim Murphy's wife, "I was manipulating your feeble little brain into doing what *I* want. What *I* want." His desire for domination over others puts them at real risk, which we see when "The Gang Buys a Boat"; he suggests to Mac that he wants the boat to take women out to the middle of nowhere, the open ocean, where they won't reject his sexual advances, "because of the implication."

Like all members of the Gang, when reality dares to challenge his fantasy, he turns extremely nasty. Tim's wife rejects him and he has a mental breakdown. "She rejected me. Me, Frank, me! The coolest guy in the history of this goddamn school! Oh, they're all gonna pay. They're all gonna pay the ultimate price!" He then reveals a hidden stash of "fetish shit" in his car, the implication being that Dennis is a repeat violent sexual offender; he may in fact have some undiagnosed antisocial personality disorder.

Cricket

In sum, the four members of the Gang all suffer from some form of self-delusion, a shared disconnection from reality. For each of them it severely reduces their own quality of life and can lead to severe problems for those unlucky enough to be around them. But, if the problem is a vice of self-delusion, then is the solution that the Gang just give-up their fantasies and return to reality? This leads us to Rickety Cricket.

Matthew 'Rickety Cricket' Mara, gives an example of the contrasting vice, that of reality without self-creation. We first meet Cricket, in "The Gang Exploits a Miracle." He was a former suitor of Dee's and on introduction, he is a priest. By exploiting his love of Dee, the Gang sets in motion a series of events that culminate in his expulsion from the church. As time passes, we see his fall from grace: Repeated exposure to the Gang causes him to be homeless, addicted to crack-cocaine, physically assaulted by the Mafia, and sexually assaulted by a dog. His life is objectively horrible.

What Cricket represents is the vice of having no dreams, no fantasy, no way out of the position he finds himself in. Catriona Mackenzie has argued in her chapter in the book *Relational Autonomy*, that a central aspect of a good moral character is the capacity to imagine oneself otherwise—in order to be autonomous and fulfilled people, we have to have some capacity to imagine our lives as different from what they are. Cricket is a great example of a defect of this capacity: After being kicked out of the church, he just gives up. Beyond the intermittent pursuit of Dee, he seems unable to hope for anything else.

Cricket, in combination with the Gang shows us the two complementary vices, two extremes that prevent a good life: As a complete disconnection from reality is detrimental to character development, so too is a life like Crickets', lived without any capacity to change. So, what do we do here? If the realms of fantasy are as bad as being crushed by reality then what should we do? We find ourselves in a dilemma. And as Aristotle suggested, a way of finding the proper path is to look for an exemplar, some person whose practical wisdom shows us how to live. Enter Frank Reynolds.

Franky Baby

We first meet Frank when "Charlie Gets Crippled": he is unhappy and wanting to reconnect with his children. "I've been manically depressed for the past couple of years and I'm not really sure what to do. . . . I just feel like I need a serious change. Or I'm gonna kill myself." What's the cause of his depression? Frank's life was disconnected from reality: "I've been asking myself the big questions recently and I realized that I don't like who your mother turned me into. The country clubs, the big house, I'm getting rid of all of it." He's been living a life that does not connect with how he sees himself.

What's important is that he recognizes this and actively wants to change. Spending a night with Mac and Charlie shows him a way to break free: "Last night was one of the best nights of my life. . . . I used to live like this. In squalor and filth. Having to scam my way through situations, getting over on people. . . . I wanna live like you again, Charlie. I wanna hang out in seedy places with degenerate characters. I wanna be pathetic. And desperate and ugly and hopeless. . . . This is the change I've been looking for!" In contrast to the hopelessness of Cricket, Frank sees another life and wants to change.

But what makes Frank different from the Gang? How can we be sure that he's not exhibiting the same vice of self-delusion? Two things show us that Frank still has some connection to reality—he's aware of what he is, and when he wants; he can still be successful. We see that he knows who he is after meeting Roxy, an alcoholic, crack-addicted prostitute, in "Frank's Pretty Woman." Frank wants to marry Roxy: "I don't care if anybody doesn't like that about me. They don't have to stick around! Screw 'em! I miss Roxy. Roxy and I are made for each other." He is under no illusions about Roxy, or about the relation between the two of them: He is not living under some delusion—not only has he chosen his given lifestyle, but he seems fairly aware of what it involves.

Perhaps more importantly, Frank is almost always successful when he wants to be. He has an almost endless source of money. He's asked to return to his old life as 'The Warthog', hard-headed business master-mind, and he shifts back into this character with ease, effortlessly making a killing. His skills at manipulating the Gang for his own benefit are second to none. He navigates his way through the world of *It's Always Sunny* with ease.

Further, if the Gang were more attentive to Frank's advice, they'd actually do a lot better themselves. The best evidence for this is where "The Gang Recycles Their Trash." After asking the Gang how many times they've attempted their hare-brained schemes, and pointing out their repeated failures, Frank states: "That's because you don't listen to me. This time we do it my way." And within minutes, we see Mac, Charlie and Dennis making thousands of dollars. And as soon as they ditch Frank's plan, they fail once more. Similarly, in "Mac and Dennis: Manhunters," Frank enrols Cricket in a (mostly) successful plan to hunt and kill Mac and Dennis. Not only does Frank succeed in his own life, but following his advice could make the Gang or Cricket successful.

Lessons Learned?

So, we can learn a lot from the Gang and Cricket. Further, we should model ourselves on Frank. Hopefully a few of you are asking "What the shit is that? Frank is a virtuous person?" Far from it. As Bruce Mathis says: "You're the little asswipe who raised my children and turned them into animals, into monsters who lie and steal and take advantage of people and contribute absolutely nothing to society."

That he charts a well-balanced path between the vices of self-delusion and hopeless reality, this alone does not make Frank a virtuous person. Indeed, the combination of characteristics makes him a truly depraved moral character, but this is not the fault of the twin vices of self-delusion or incapacity to change. Probably being put in a nitwit school and falling in love with a lipless frog kid didn't help him though.

9
The D.E.N.N.I.S System

ROGER HUNT

One question that plagues some philosophers and certainly those who don't study philosophy is: what do philosophers do? Lacking the ability to resist such questions of self-reflective import, philosophers have provided a variety of answers. I'll answer this question through the D.E.N.N.I.S System.

But First . . .

The classic distinction in the history of philosophy which every undergrad writes about is between empiricism and rationalism. Empiricists start philosophical reasoning from perceptions of the world. The scientific method draws considerable influence from this tradition.

The goal of empiricism is to construct answers to the Big questions starting by exploring what is in the world. David Hume worked this way starting his philosophical treatise from an analysis of how our sensations of the world become ideas, how those ideas become concepts, and how—or if—we can construct true theories from those concepts.

As it happens, Hume concluded that we should be skeptical of any theory derived in this way since there is no way for us to know, or sense the basic principles—causation, space, and time—with which we intuitively reason about the world. I always think of Frank as an empiricist, since he started living with Charlie to be in squalor like he used to. I think of him as leaving the comfort of relying on principles and structure in favor of experiencing the truth a.k.a. the messiness of the world. Even though he may wear a suit and run a multi-million dollar investment firm, they still call him "the Warthog" and he relies on gritty tactics to succeed. The "rationality" of his previous life was just a cover for what is basically street hustling.

Rationalists, on the other hand, start reasoning from first principles, or statements which cannot possibly be doubted, and try to derive the rest of knowledge from those statements. René Descartes works this way, starting his analysis from the only statement he cannot doubt, namely that he in fact exists. From this indubitable premise, he goes on to derive a proof of God's existence, the foundations of analytic geometry, and a theory of cosmology, just to name a few. If I had to choose a character who exemplifies rationalism—and it potential pitfalls—it would have to be Mac. He is constantly taking a principle which he is completely sure of and reasons from it to a solution for whatever issue is facing him that day.

These approaches might be called prescriptivist, as they prescribe how philosophy should be done. Another way of thinking about philosophical method is to describe what philosophers actually do. This is sometimes called the dialectic method. Thought of in this way, philosophers work by comparing opposing arguments and in most cases take the best parts of each argument to derive a mutually acceptable conclusion. Doing this often requires dialogue, so philosophers sometimes present their work as a narrative. Plato's work, for instance, is presented like a recording of a discussion between Socrates and someone else. Rather than reasoning from experience or first principles, Socrates questions other people's beliefs to determine whether or not they are justified in holding them. His goal is to find answers which hold up to such scrutiny.

It Starts with "D" and Ends with "ennis"

The D.E.N.N.I.S system is Dennis's methodology for doing whatever it is he does to women, and it's a particularly apt—though disparaging—description of how philosophers actually work. It includes some very compelling suggestions for how philosophers should approach and ultimately resolve, or in some cases abandon philosophical problems.

The D.E.N.N.I.S system, according to Dennis, allows him to "seduce any woman and earn her undying love." One or two interesting things to say on this point. The term "philosophy" derives from the Greek term "Sophia" which also refers to the Greek Goddess of Wisdom. So we could think of trying to understand philosophy like trying to understand a Goddess. Extending this a bit, we could think of pursuing philosophy kind of like seducing someone—it's debatable whether or not truly understanding philosophy or truly seducing someone is possible. Some philosophers even liken studying philosophy to interacting with someone, typically a woman given that men dominated thought for so many millennia.

Boethius, a sixth-century Roman philosopher locked away for political reasons, narrates an encounter with Philosophy, a female spirit, reflects on dialogues with her, and her teaching and love consoles him through a dire set of circumstances. Presentations like this reveal philosophy as an encounter, rather than just mulling things over alone in an ivory tower.

So, if philosophy is thought of as similar to seducing a woman, which certainly reflects the difficulty of philosophical questions, what can we learn from the D.E.N.N.I.S system?

"D"emonstrative Value

In the show, Dennis accomplishes this with Caley, his love interest a.k.a. mark a.k.a. philosophical problem, by recognizing she is a pharmacist, and he pretends to purchase medication for his grandmother by showing (or lying about) his sympathetic demeanor and capacity to care for others. This is a particular kind of value, one not specific to seducing women. Let's assume that as philosophers we are not lying about our intentions, understanding a problem in terms of its history, its current status, and the kinds of approaches likely to provide some insight into it is extremely important. Not only do we as philosophers need to show that we are worthy of approaching such a problem, but we also have to take care to demonstrate how valuable the problem is to itself. One of the first things we do in a philosophy article is explain why this problem is important, and pay it respect by demonstrating what make us capable of handling it.

The Gang provides some of their own ideas about what it means to demonstrate value. Charlie, for instance, tries to demonstrate his value to the waitress by clogging her sink with hair, then hoping she will invite him over—or more likely he imagines himself just showing up—to fix it for her. Dennis strikes this down, as it obviously fails, but let me try to elucidate why. First, Charlie chose an approach which he could never fulfill. He even failed to get the hair in there. So how could he get it out? He wasn't aware of what makes him valuable, thus he would obviously fail to seduce the waitress/solve the problem.

Second, he is creating an issue, hair in the sink, which doesn't concern the waitress, and which she likely wouldn't call him for anyway. This is an important lesson for young philosophers: do not bite off more than you can chew, so to speak. Dennis's suggestion to Charlie is to go where the waitress works, the carnival, and demonstrate his value by winning her a prize; not bad and perhaps even within Charlie's range. He still may not succeed, but at least he may see some progress. Dee also presents a scenario of asserting her independence, which Dennis immediately strikes down. Instead, he raises the issue that Dee has no value. What is a philosopher of no value to do? Well, he suggests she lower Ben's value by making out with a carney . . . sometimes when a problem is too difficult we can rethink it as something less difficult. Philosophy professors do this on exams all the time!

In these senses, the D is a pretty good description of how philosophers approach philosophical problems: understand the problem and our own capacity to present an enlightening discussion of it.

"E"ngage Physically

For Dennis, this means getting the mark back to the apartment by taking her to a restaurant that is closed, and suggesting they go back to his place with a pizza and movie, Mac is the wing man with his "I saw a spider so I need to use the living room" routine, and Dennis gets her onto his bed.

First, although we definitely like to think of philosophical problems as purely intellectually, working on them definitely takes a physical toll. Lowering sleep, drinking too much caffeine, relaxing with too much beer, smoking too many cigarettes, pulling out hair . . . the works. So to think of philosophy as a physical endeavor is definitely accurate.

Second, actually having sex and actually doing philosophy aren't that far removed. Hear me out. Many people think of philosophy as kind of wise sayings, or clever turns of phrase: you're not in traffic, you are traffic. These interesting bits of thought which entertain us for a little bit definitely aren't doing philosophy. It's kind of like fantasizing about doing philosophy. It seem wondrous and mystical. Kind of like fantasizing about sex, and that magical moment. More often than not, however, sex doesn't actually work that way. Oftentimes it is quite awkward, messy, and unsatisfying, with exceptions obviously. The reason it's so difficult at times is that many things can happen which aren't planned on . . . won't go into details. This happens in philosophy as well. Doing philosophy is a dragging slog of examining logic, and struggling to come up with counterexamples to premises. It can be unbelievably messy and unsatisfying, with some exceptions of course. What I'm trying to say is that without some kind of carnal investment, the D.E.N.N.I.S system fails, just like doing philosophy fails without some kind of trollish jaunt through premise after premise. One final comparison:

things may be going along very well for a little while, but one wrong move and you have to start all over again as if all the great work you just did is now for not . . . philosophy is the same way. Essentially, you have to get down and dirty with a philosophy problem to make any progress. Okay, I'm done.

"N"urture That Dependence

This is probably the most difficult step of the philosophical process for those who don't study philosophy, or even those who do but maybe never had to write a thesis. Most students of philosophy in with the D and E very well, as writing a philosophy paper absolutely requires an attempt to understand the issue and get deep into the logic of he the arguments. However, writing a response or even a term paper typically ends there, just as perhaps some are content with a successful sexual conquest (men and women are guilty of this, I'm sure!). The real difficulty in philosophy comes when you have to let your work sit, boil, and most likely fester in your mind. Just as Dennis is able to fester in the minds of his victims. His approach is to simulate an angry neighbor threatening to kill the mark, so that she will be so emotionally distraught so as to become even more connected to him than she thought possible. Philosophy problems do this to as well. You finish the first draft of a forty-page master's thesis, or dissertation chapter, you rest for a few days while your advisor reads it, and suddenly your argument seems to disgust you, you feel sick, you figure you've completely failed, wasted several months and will never finish and your life will be over! Then, hopefully gently, your advisor takes you into her office, she douses you in praise and some helpful criticism, the path to finishing seems brighter, and before you know it you're back into the thick of things, finding more effective phrasing, and maybe a brilliant reformulation of the argument. (Your) philosophy was freaking out on you, but with some careful coaching you were able to rein things in, calming each other down and getting ready to settle in for a few month, maybe even years of intellectual bliss.

"N"eglect Emotionally

You're three quarters of the way through the thesis, and all of a sudden nothing seems to be working. It's a very similar anxiety as before, but this time your advisor can do nothing to save you. Writer's block running rampant, you just read a new article in *Philosophical Inquiry* which not only resembles your idea, but is also way more effectively presented, and even worse, ultimately rejected by the author in favor of what seems like a way more plausible position. You and philosophy are touring each other.

You take a trip to India using your university credit and what's left of the money your parents gave you for completing undergrad. You're sure some time in the mountains, or seeing an elephant, or learning tantric yoga will clear your mind, but it just ends up being a week of dysentery and horrible air quality. You consider quitting philosophy and becoming a spice salesman or even stealing someone of the those blind children from the local king pin and starting an oasis safe from any professional journal, and you can create a master race of brilliant deformed people who will slink across the earth spreading wisdom from the safety of street corners and sleeping on heating grates in the winter.

"I"nspire Hope

Suddenly the realization washes over you that all you have to do is finish this damn thing. It's no magnum opus, but hey, who cares, it's just for a degree, right? You stumble back from an exhausting trip, crack down, crank it out, give it a quasi proof, your advisor looks less than amazed, you ask if she will sign it, she reluctantly says yes. You set a defense date. Philosophy couldn't be more pleased to get ready to admit you to the ranks. Now this engagement with philosophy is the best of all because it's really emotional for her. She lets you do whatever you want; all of your arguments and responses to objections seem brilliant. Nothing could be going better . . . Little does philosophy know . . .

"S"eparate Entirely

You've spent a good amount of time preparing for the dissertation committee's objections, you make your presentation, squeak by, they sign, and you slink off into the night never to be heard of again. And the best part is you've set it up so that you can get this problem back whenever you want. You've made a professional contribution, and caused serious trauma to a problem which once stood dauntingly in front of you.

MAC: Move in After Completion

However, while you may be finished with it for now, your friend on the couch with the spider routine wearing glasses and reading and shit discovers an opening in your argument, blogs about it, and everyone secretly makes fun of what a ridiculous argument you made, but you don't care because you're on to the next issue.

Scraps

Then, packing a wad of hundreds and some magnum condoms, Mantis feasts! Or, you condense your thesis to a "smart thinking" book or give a TED talk.

So, what's it like to do philosophy? That pretty much sums it up. How should you do philosophy? Be a sociopath about it.

IV

Morals

10
Yes Means Yes, Unless It Means No

Tim Aylsworth

In "The Gang Buys a Boat," Dennis and Mac go out to gather some supplies (like "slacks and docksiders" to get the right look). While they're in the hardware store, Dennis casually mentions that they still need to get a mattress—preferably a nice one. This comes as a surprise to Mac, who innocently asks why they need a mattress. Dennis explains that the *whole point* of buying the boat was to take women out on the water, "get them nice and tipsy topside," and then have sex with them.

He figures that this plan is bound to work, of course, since he'll be making these ladies an "offer" that they can't refuse. Dennis (being the borderline sociopath that he is) reveals the sinister plan like it's no big deal. He tells Mac that the women can't *really* say no . . . "because of the implication." As he puts it, they will think to themselves, "I'm out in the middle of nowhere with some dude I barely know. I look around and what do I see? Nothing but open ocean. Ahhh, there's nowhere for me to run, what am I gonna do, say no?"

Mac begins to pick up on the fact that it sort of "sounds like these women don't want to have sex" with Dennis at all. Mac even asks Dennis if he's "going to hurt women." Mac thinks that the implication of rape or violence "seems really dark" (even for Dennis), but Dennis rather indignantly replies that he doesn't see it like that. After all, he retorts,

113

"If the girl said no, then the answer obviously is no. But the thing is that she's not gonna say no, she would never say no . . . because of *the implication*." As Mac presses him on what he means by "the implication," Dennis explains that it's the "implication that things might go wrong for her if she refuses to sleep with me. Now, not that things are gonna go wrong for her, but she's thinking that they will."

This scene is delightfully dark, and it deals with a topic that most shows would never touch. It's also the perfect backdrop for a philosophical discussion about the nature of sexual consent—an important ethical issue. Although everyone would agree that non-consensual sex (rape) is a serious moral wrong, some people disagree about exactly what constitutes "consent."

No Means No

We're all familiar with the principle that "no means no." And rightly so. "No" does *not* mean "keep going until I say yes," "pressure me into saying yes," "convince me to say yes," or anything of the kind. "No" absolutely and unequivocally means no, and any sex that happens after someone says "no" is rape.

From what he says to Mac, it sounds like Dennis agrees with this principle. If the woman says no, then the answer is no. But in his mind, this seems to imply something else. Understanding it as the converse of the rule that "No means no," Dennis figures that "Yes means yes." He thinks that if the woman on the boat says "yes" (even because of an implication of violence), then she has consented to having sex with him. Of course, the viewers (and the horrified onlooker in the hardware store) know that Dennis is wrong. If the woman on the boat doesn't resist Dennis's advances simply because she fears for her safety, then her "Yes" doesn't really constitute consent.

Thus we arrive at our philosophical problem. Not every "Yes" counts as consent. But if that's true, then how should we define sexual consent? As luck would have it, members of the Gang find themselves in a variety of situations which will help us work out the answer to this question.

Rather than looking at cases where consent is clearly obtained, we'll look at some of the more problematic ones. We'll come to understand what consent *is* by first understanding what it *isn't*. As we'll see, there are all kinds of different situations where consent either is not or cannot be given (such as when someone is underage, when someone is extremely drunk, or when someone is mentally disabled). Once we realize why consent is impossible in these cases, we will have worked out a definition of consent. Or, to use some terms that philosophers like to throw around, we will have established the necessary and sufficient conditions for consent.

Why Sex with Children Is Wrong

One of the most obvious cases where saying "yes" is not sufficient for consent is an adult having sex with a child. Indeed, most people consider sex with children to be an especially horrific moral wrong. Not only is it rape, but the rape takes place at a particularly vulnerable time in someone's development—childhood.

Although it's not the same thing as child molestation, the Gang does explore the issue of statutory rape in "Underage Drinking: A National Concern." But, fortunately for the moral comfort of the viewers, Dennis and Dee planned to go to a prom (and possibly have sex with) high school seniors rather than younger children. Even so, Sweet Dee can't help but hesitate when she's in the car with Trey, because, as she puts it, she's "never statutory raped anyone before."

Things are a bit different, however, with Dennis and Tammy. When Tammy is throwing herself at Dennis she says to him, "Dude, relax. I'm eighteen . . . I'm legal, and I *love* to party" (this is *classic* Tammy). Even Mac and Charlie change their tune when they find out she's eighteen. They tell Dennis, "You're a lucky man. Eighteen is legal, bro. *This isn't a morality contest.*"

But what if Tammy and Trey weren't eighteen-year-old seniors? What if instead they were fourteen-year-old freshmen? Then I think we would view Dennis and Dee in a wholly different light. Even if a fourteen-year-old Tammy came up to Dennis in the same way and was completely willing to have sex with him, it would still be statutory rape.

Of course, our concern wouldn't be limited to the illegality of the act. Sure, Dennis having sex with a fourteen-year-old would be illegal, but more importantly, *it would be immoral*. So in order to answer the initial question about what consent is, we should ask why we think it's immoral for an adult to have sex with a fourteen-year-old.

What makes it morally wrong for a grown man to have sex with a "willing" fourteen-year old girl is that a fourteen-year-old *isn't capable of giving fully-informed consent*. Even if she's saying that she wants to have sex with an adult, she isn't mature enough to fully understand her actions.

The reason that young children can't give consent is that we don't think that their intellectual capacities are sufficient for them to understand the decision or to be fully informed about sex and its potential consequences. They can't yet understand the rightness or wrongness of the action in question. To use one more piece of philosophy jargon, we would say the child is not yet a full-blown "moral agent."

This concept of moral agency is useful because it helps us to distinguish between people and things that we can hold accountable. If a tree falls and hits me on the head, it would be ridiculous for me to hold the tree morally responsible or to blame it for what happened. On the other hand, if some guy punches me in the face for no reason, I can and will hold him accountable. The jabroni who punched me is a moral agent and the tree is not.

It's a bit more complicated when a five-year-old punches me in the face. It might simply be that the child doesn't yet understand that it's wrong to punch people in the face. And so we think that the child isn't really a moral agent yet. It's similar when a cat scratches me. I don't hold the cat responsible because I don't think it's a moral agent either. Since young children aren't moral agents, who are capable of fully understanding the consequences or moral rightness of their actions, they can't consent to sex with adults (nor can cats for that matter). This is why you shouldn't have sex with children . . . or cats.

Intellectual Disabilities and Consent

Children and animals aren't the only ones who are incapable of giving sexual consent. In the episode, "Sweet Dee's Dating a Retarded Person," we have to face the possibility of another relationship where sexual consent might be impossible. If children lack the cognitive capacities to understand sex well enough to give fully-informed consent, then the intellectually disabled also lack this capacity. (Important side note: Although "intellectually disabled" is an unfamiliar term to most people and it's bit awkward to say, I avoid using the word 'retarded' except in direct quotations. But, to be clear, the label "intellectually disabled" refers to what used to be called "mentally retarded." So I'm talking about people with an IQ below 70, who have *significant* intellectual limitations. I'm not talking about folks like Charlie, who are just a bit slow.)

Throughout the episode, Dennis tries to convince Dee that Lil' Kev is "an actual retarded person." And Dennis has several points in his favor: Kevin is drooling on himself in his yearbook picture, he lives with his mom, his shirt is on backwards, he doesn't drive, and the nail in the coffin is the way that he laughs uncontrollably at a childish cartoon while sloppily shoving popcorn into his mouth. So Dee gives in. She begins to think that Lil' Kev is indeed mentally handicapped. Not only would it be humiliating for her to be gold-digging someone who is intellectually disabled, it would almost certainly be a moral wrong. So Sweet Dee does what she thinks is the right thing and breaks up with him.

It turns out, however, that Dennis was wrong. In a well-executed freestyle rap Lil' Kev demonstrates that his cognitive capacities are fully intact:

Lookin' like a zombie
Walkin' like a chicken
Mouth is full of shit
That's why her breath be stinkin'
Just one question Dee
Before ya take your bow
Your gravy train's leavin'
So who's retarded now?

Once again, it'll be useful for us to imagine how we'd feel if things had turned out differently. What if Lil' Kevin *was* intellectually disabled? I think most people would say that having sex with such a person is morally reprehensible. To put it mildly, it's taking advantage of someone, or to put it less mildly, it's rape.

The issue here is pretty much the same as the case of sex with children. It doesn't matter whether or not the intellectually disabled person said "yes." The idea is that this person lacks the cognitive capacities required for fully-informed consent. Thus it would be morally wrong to have sex with someone who's intellectually disabled.

I think the best explanation we can give of these moral intuitions has something to do with cognitive capacities and the ability to understand the decision. If someone is not able to fully understand what's going on, then they can't consent to it.

And so our definition of consent will require that the agreement to have sex be made by "fully-informed, competent moral agents." This rules out the possibility of children and the intellectually disabled consenting to sex. It also rules out the possibility of consensual sex with someone who's extremely drunk. And that's the topic of the next section.

Sex with the Extremely Intoxicated

If sexual consent requires a certain level of cognitive functioning in order for moral agents to be fully informed, then those who are extremely intoxicated are also unable to consent. Unsurprisingly, the Gang has had plenty of experiences with people who are extremely intoxicated.

When "The Gang Goes to the Jersey Shore," Charlie has his first and only romantic night with the Waitress. But, when she wakes up, she tells him that she was on MDMA and that she has no memory of what happened. She says, "Oh my God! Charlie. What the . . . ? *Did you rape me last night?* Why am I waking up next to you on a deserted beach? I was on ecstasy last night. You have to tell me everything that happened."

Notice how she didn't ask "did you have sex with me last night?" The reason she chose the word 'rape' is that she was so intoxicated that *she wouldn't have been able to consent to sex.* Her cognitive capacities were so limited from the drugs that any sex that took place would've been non-consensual.

Here's a pretty common refrain that you'll hear from anyone who's familiar with the concept of date-rape (which, by the way, is an *unacceptably* common occurrence, especially on college campuses): *drunken consent is not consent.* If one person is sober, and the other person is extremely drunk, then the sex that takes place is not consensual *even if the drunk person says yes.*

At the Halloween party, Charlie, Dennis, Mac, and Dee were all thoroughly hammered. If one of the McPoyle brothers, sober from drinking warm milk all night, were to have had sex with Dennis, then it would most certainly be rape (fortunately for him, the McPoyles usually like to keep it in the family). Dennis was too drunk to consent to sex, and if he was in his right mind, he would never have sex with a McPoyle. Well . . . he wouldn't have sex with a McPoyle unless he were held hostage by them and he thought it would be a way out of the situation. And that brings me to my final point.

Sex, Power, and Implications of Violence

When "The Gang Gets Held Hostage," everyone starts to panic. Dee and Charlie come down with "a nasty case of Stockholm Syndrome," and the Gang smashes much of the bar to pieces. The McPoyles had them at gunpoint, and tensions were running high. So Dennis devises a plan to sneak out. He tells Dee that he can get Margaret McPoyle to fall in love with him: "I just need to get alone with her. Let the pecks do the talking. One thing will lead to the next; she'll lead me secretly to safety."

And when he takes Margaret to the bathroom, it certainly seems like Dennis is consenting to the sex. He says to her, "You're a stone cold fox, and I want you. I gotta have you. I need you. I want you inside me." That sure sounds like consent to me. If we took it out of context, I think that such expressions would certainly count as consent. But that's the rub. Context matters. If you're being held at gunpoint, and you offer sex to get out of the situation, then saying "yes" doesn't count as consent.

So if Dennis had sex with Margaret, we could say that he was raped. Luckily for Dennis, it doesn't look like they had sex, it was just some steamy, passionate, milky kissing. Nevertheless, the kissing was non-consensual . . . and pretty gross.

Thus, our definition of consent will need a clause indicating that the agreement must take place beforehand in a context where the agents can freely express their genuine preferences. A hostage situation is awfully far from one in which you can freely express yourself. Thus, consent cannot be given in such a situation.

Now we're coming full circle. This is precisely what I think is going on in the "implication" scene. The idea behind Dennis's plan is that the women won't say no because they will fear for their safety. As he said, "it's the implication that things might go wrong for her if she refuses to sleep with me." If the woman is in a dangerous situation and she says yes simply because she fears that Dennis will rape and murder her if she says no, then she is not really consenting.

We could imagine many similar situations where power dynamics or implications of possible harm would affect someone's capacity to freely express their desires. If a prison guard tells a prisoner that she will be spared hard labor or time in solitary confinement on the condition that she has sex with him, then her "yes" doesn't count as consent. If a boss tells his secretary that she'll be fired if she doesn't have sex with him, then the possibility of genuine consent is compromised.

I could go on listing examples forever. But, at this point, I think I should respond to an objection you might have. You might say that the woman on the boat *is* freely expressing herself. She can freely choose between a. having sex with Dennis and b. facing the possibility of being raped and murdered. It's her call. And, in the hostage situation, Dennis can freely choose between a. milky kissing with Margaret McPoyle or b. returning to the hostage situation. The prisoner can choose either a. sex with the guard or b. time in solitary confinement. These are "free" choices; no one is physically forcing them to have sex. So you might think it's unfair of me to claim that these choices don't qualify as consent.

I concede that these scenarios all involve choices. But there's something very wrong with the way these choices are set up. If the woman on the boat chooses sex with Dennis so as to avoid the possibility of being murdered at sea, then the choice doesn't really reflect her true preferences. She might prefer sex with Dennis over death, but, more importantly, she would prefer *not to be in that situation at all*. The same goes for the prisoner or for Dennis in the hostage situation. Dennis might prefer sex with Margaret over being held at gunpoint, but his genuine preference is to not be confronted with that decision in the first place.

So, when I said that consent requires that the agents be able to "freely express their genuine preferences," this is what I think is at stake. When you're facing an implication of violence or harm, you aren't free to express your true preferences. Thus, Mac was quite astute to pick up on how Dennis was making it "sound like she doesn't want to have sex" with him at all. She might *say* that she wants to have sex with him, but if she's only saying that because she fears for her life, then it doesn't count as consent because that's not her true preference.

It's Mutual, Baby

I've argued that sexual consent is an agreement between moral agents who have adequately functioning cognitive capacities. This requires that they not be children, intellectually disabled, or extremely intoxicated. I've also argued that consent cannot take place when someone fears for their safety.

So after seeing the many ways that consent can go wrong, we're finally ready for the definition. From what's been said, I think we should define sexual consent as a mutual, explicit agreement between fully-informed, competent moral agents to perform some sexual act, and the agreement must take place beforehand in a context where the agents can freely express their genuine preferences.

That definition might sound a bit complicated, but it really isn't. I think we all have strong moral intuitions about what consent is. And most of those intuitions are spot on. But sometimes it's a good idea to make those intuitions more precise by looking at examples and getting clear about what's going on with the concept in question.

In the end, consent shouldn't be a terribly difficult concept. But it's an important one. Sex without consent is rape, and rape is a serious moral wrong. So it's a good idea for us to develop a solid understanding of what's required for someone to consent to sex. And it looks like Dennis has some work to do on that front. It's a good thing Mac was there to call him out for being such a shady jabroni.

11
The Gang Gets Pardoned

ETHAN CHAMBERS

The five central characters of *It's Always Sunny* are terrible people. Each member of the Gang is a narcissistic, greedy, unstable asshole with few, if any, redeeming qualities. However there might be philosophical doubts about *why* they are like this. We might wonder whether, given their circumstances, we could reasonably expect them to turn out any other way. If we can't, then maybe we should stop blaming and despising the Gang and start feeling sorry for them.

David Hume was an eighteenth-century philosopher whose writings on ethics and metaphysics can help us view assholes in a more sympathetic light. So let's look at each member of the Gang in turn, and see whether Hume's approach to ethics can help us to explain them, and even forgive them.

King of the Rats

Charlie highlights the way the argument works better than any other member of the Gang. If we delve into his complicated psyche we can see that he is composed of both virtues and vices, two key components of Hume's ethical theory. Virtues are the good, moral elements of someone's character while vices are the opposite, and everyone possesses at least some of both, but what's strange about Charlie is that he often displays totally contradictory character traits, sometimes in the same episode. For example when we see Charlie feeling upset about slaughtering rats we believe that he has the virtue of compassion, while his glee at getting to kill more rats later on makes us accuse him of the vice of cruelty.

Despite this, Charlie comes across as generally likeable, which I don't believe comes down to the fact that his virtues outweigh his vices—far from it, Charlie once nearly killed all of his friends just to prove that he's a "wild card" ("The Gang Solves the Gas Crisis"). Instead I believe that the audience understands why Charlie has the vices he does, and is thus able to tolerate them. Hume expressed this in philosophical terms by outlining what we now call the "causal theory of the self"—the theory that psychological laws are just as rigid as physical laws. Just as the laws of physics dictate that what goes up must come down, the laws of human psychology dictate that if your mother prostitutes herself on Christmas Day while you sniff glue, you'll probably grow up with some problems.

Charlie's dire existence is what makes us repeatedly forgive his faults. Knowing about Charlie's traumatic childhood lets us in on his mind's inner "causal story," the chain of events that led from, say, his abuse by Uncle Jack to his inability to connect with the waitress without breaking the law. This story is easy to tell with faults that aren't strictly moral, for example Charlie's illiteracy, an intellectual fault, is explained by a poor education. Similarly his other vices, such as his substance abuse problems, are clearly explained by his exposure to drugs at an early age, just as his moral vice of racism stems from ignorance of the world outside Philadelphia. If we see these psychological causes leading directly to psychological effects, it becomes easier to view Charlie as a victim of circumstance and harder to blame him.

Knowing why Charlie is the way he is relies on our ability to exercise "sympathy"—a term that David Hume used to mean something more like what we call empathy—the ability to be able to step into someone else's shoes and wonder if we would act any differently. Everyone knows a kid at school that 'just never stood a chance'. Charlie Kelly was one of those kids. Abused, undereducated and thrust into a life of squalor, Charlie was never taught the social or moral rules that now come naturally to most people. "A Very Sunny Christmas" offers us one of the few sentimental moments in the show when we see a young Mac and Charlie throwing rocks at trains, having nowhere else to go on Christmas Day because of their terrible parents. I believe that seeing scenes like these make it easier to sympathize with a character like Charlie, and that if we expand on this reasoning we can exonerate the rest of the gang as well.

Ronnie the Rat

What are the character traits that play a role in the psychological causality of Mac's mind? For one, he's completely deluded. Almost totally ignorant of the Bible and its teachings, Mac somehow sees himself sitting at the right hand of God when he dies ("The Gang Saves the Day"). No matter how many times Mac runs away from danger, or gets beaten up, or poops himself when threatened, he still believes himself to be a capable fighter. Despite his relationship with Carmen and increasingly obvious homosexual overtones, Mac fails to face up to his own sexuality. These delusions in themselves are easy enough to understand—Mac leads a wretched life and wants to pretend that he's better than he is. What the story of Mac also highlights is that psychological causality isn't just about looking back to what caused our vices; it can also be about looking forward to see what might inspire our virtues.

Mac was bullied just like Charlie in high school; a traumatizing enough experience as it is, but Mac was bullied for trying to be good. "Ronnie the Rat" would tell the teachers when other students were up to trouble and got nothing but scorn and resentment for it. At home, Mac saw his father deal drugs and steal Christmases with the result that Mac got money and toys. Without ever seeing the value of virtue, nothing ever caused Mac to develop an inclination to do the right thing.

The city of Philadelphia—at least as presented in the show—is almost exclusively filled with wrongdoers and criminals who lead fairly successful lives. Given this, can we really judge Mac for the way he behaves, seeing as it earns him a comfortable living as Dennis's sidekick? In his position, would we try to do the right thing, knowing perfectly well that everyone around us would take advantage of us as a result? It seems likely that any of us, dropped into this fictional Philly, would soon learn that it's a pound or get pounded situation.

If there's any moral to be taken from watching *It's Always Sunny*, it's that good people suffer for their goodness. Anyone who encounters the Gang learns this lesson soon enough. When we first meet "Rickety Cricket" he seems like a nice guy, but repeated encounters with the toxic gang have seen him stabbed, shot, and possibly burned alive. He goes from a priest to a drug dealer to a thief to a dog executioner because he soon sees that the world of *It's Always Sunny* isn't made for priests—it's made for scheming scumbags like the Gang.

Despite this, Ronnie the Rat continues trying to do the right thing, even if only when it benefits him and even if Mac's interpretation of 'do the right thing' is 'arbitrarily obey Bible fragments'. Mac's malformed morality is easily traceable back to his monosyllabic mother, who apparently at least tried to teach Mac right from wrong before her speech devolved into meaningless grunts. If I'm right, this traumatic childhood, and traumatic adulthood, inevitably shaped a naive little boy into the jerk we know and love. Hume might say that we can no more blame Mac for being a bad man than we can blame *Lethal Weapon 6* for being a bad movie—that's just the way they're made.

The Golden God

The arguments that save Dennis from moral responsibility are perhaps less obvious than the other gang members. He's from a wealthy background, so it's not like he never stood a chance. He's at least more intelligent than the others, so we can't say that he just doesn't know any better when he commits evil acts. He just seems plain nasty–a misogynistic, sociopathic, rage-fuelled asshole so vain he may actually believe himself to be a god. What story of psychological causation could possibly warrant this behavior?

Some aspects of his personality can be seen as a typical reaction to childhood trauma. We know his parents were unaffectionate to the point of cruelty—recall Frank buying the twins the gifts they wanted just to snatch them away again. This childhood, followed by an adolescence in which he was likely ignored at school, even if he doesn't realize it, could have led Dennis to a kind of Mac-like delusion in which he is the golden god and everyone else merely savages.

This would be bad enough, but things get worse for Dennis—when he grows up he starts to see those delusions being confirmed. He can cope ridiculously well in the world of *It's Always Sunny*; despite putting in no effort and being completely amoral he owns and runs a bar that does well enough to provide him with a comfortable existence. Add to this his frequent success with women and we see that Dennis is perfectly adapted to the terrible world around him. Lacking any real goal, Dennis has achieved everything he wanted to by his thirties. And the people around him *are* ignorant savages; the McPoyles, his family, his friends, all are just as ignorant and awful as Dennis believes. The only problem is that he fails to lump himself in with them—when we see him destroying a man's bathroom in "The Gang Reignites the Rivalry," he complains about the rudeness of others as he does so. Dennis literally cannot see how those same objections might apply to him.

Other characters react to the Gang in similar fashion— the nicest man in the show, Bruce Mathis, gets genuine pleasure out of saving and raising orphaned children. But when he sees the animals his own children have become, he shows immoral behavior towards them, trying to get Dee and Frank to have sex to catch them out in their own manipulation in "Dennis and Dee's Mom Is Dead." Similarly the lawyer repeatedly harms the gang, but these characters are let off the hook, as we know that they're generally good people; it's only in reaction to the Gang that they exhibit their own vices. We let them off the hook because the Gang deserve it, but perhaps Dennis's actions stem from the fact that he feels everybody else deserves it too—and most of the time, he's right. Of course, any real person acting like Dennis couldn't defend themselves in this way; it's only in the comically cruel Philadelphia where Dennis lives that Hume's philosophy could even possibly excuse his actions.

What else motivates Dennis's behavior? In "Charlie's Mom Has Cancer" Dennis claims that he cannot feel feelings, and this certainly seems to be true; apart from rage and sometimes disappointment when he fails, Dennis experiences few emotions. This is easily explained; Dennis's grandfather was a Nazi, his father was Frank, and his mother was Frank's "whore wife," hardly an environment likely to foster a healthy emotional system.

If it's true that Dennis can't feel feelings then he can't possibly feel sympathy, for Hume a key factor in helping us determine what is right. And this is why we can't fully blame him for his evil deeds. It isn't that Dennis chooses not to feel anything; it's that his upbringing and resulting psychological disorders have left him unable to feel even if he wants to. Dennis cannot even step on the first rung of the ethical ladder; just as we don't blame a cat for chasing mice, how can we blame Dennis for treating others the way he does? Free will is a tricky concept, so it's difficult to argue that Dennis has *no* choice in his actions, but we could argue that, lacking the ability to know how others feel and the desire to find out, moral options simply will not occur to Dennis in the first place.

The Aluminum Monster

If we can find sympathy with Mac and Charlie, and at least come to understand Dennis, can we find pity for Dee? Her upbringing was as heinous as Dennis's, if not more so—Dee's mother once claimed that she, yet not her twin Dennis, was a mistake. Years stuck in a debilitating back brace that led to constant abuse mean that we perhaps feel pity for Dee more than the others. Too often the joke is on Dee, and the audience is encouraged to think even less of the Gang when they relentlessly torment her.

So it might be worth remembering that Dee can be the worst of the lot. She regularly threatens to destroy her enemies, and makes new enemies just as frequently. She quickly asserts her dominance over weaker characters, trying to belittle Fatty McGoo and Rickety Cricket so that she can feel better about herself, even when she knows how hurtful bullying is. Hopefully she will illustrate my point—audience members usually feel sorry for Dee more than anything, even when she's at her most vitriolic. Shouldn't we use the same logic for the rest of the gang, even if their sympathetic reasons are not as obvious as Deandra's?

We can easily see Dee's causal story being that the gang acting obnoxiously to Dee leads directly to her reacting with fury and taking it out on others. But this is only half the tale; the gang themselves are motivated by the cruelty done to them, and the characters who suffer from that, including Cricket and The Lawyer, soon turn nasty themselves to settle the score. It's easy to believe that in different circumstances, Dee could have turned out alright but alas, she was born to . . .

The Warthog

We can now directly or indirectly trace the warped character of the Reynolds twins to Frank's terrible parenting, and could possibly trace Charlie's abandonment issues to his absentee (potential) father. So is Frank the root of all evil? He warps the Gang, who in turn warp each other and the world around them, before Frank returns to the Gang and exacerbates the situation for all of them?

If we look at Frank with the same critical eye we have used on the others, we see that this is not the whole story. In fact Frank, having the most traumatic childhood of all, may be the easiest to exempt from full moral culpability. We know from "The Gang Gets Analyzed" that Frank spent part of his childhood in a draconian mental institution, on suspicion of suffering from "donkey brains," where he shared his first kiss with another patient known only as "the Frog Girl."

There's always the possibility that this account of Frank's childhood is untrue. Yet assuming for the moment that it's not, it actually seems a minor miracle that Frank turned out as well as he has. We might expect a child spending any amount of time in such horrible conditions to be socially stunted for life; instead Frank started a business, married, and raised two children. Yes, the business was crooked, the marriage a train wreck, and the children vicious monsters, but that's still more than most of the characters in the *It's Always Sunny* universe achieve.

Now let's look at the other possibility: this history is untrue and Frank's childhood wasn't as traumatic as he claims. Given that he tells his tale to a psychoanalyst, a person he has no reason to deceive, in total privacy, it seems unlikely that he's lying about this. He also has a perfectly legitimate medical certificate clearing him of having donkey brain. If he's not lying, yet we still believe his story to be untrue, only one possibility remains: Frank is completely insane.

This option looks like a winner, whether we believe the "donkey brain" tale or not. Frank exhibits suicidal tendencies, severe memory loss, and frequent mental breakdowns. In "Mac and Charlie Die (Part 2)," Frank carries around a stuffed doll representing Charlie and apparently "bangs" it; hardly the behavior of a well man. Whether we blame his age, his incarceration, his drug abuse, or his continued exposure to the Gang, there's little doubt that Frank is completely out of his mind for most of the show's run. Mental illness is one of the strongest arguments against someone's moral responsibility; if a person cannot correctly interpret the world around them, or if their character is radically altered by the illness, then their power to affect their own psychological causal story is in doubt. Any choices they make or actions they perform are caused by the illness, and would not necessarily be endorsed by their healthy selves. Frank's just another link in the chain of bad behavior and abuse, from the assholes that broke the Liberty Bell down to the assholes that produce "The Nightman Cometh."

The Gang Gets Justified

Looking at the world in light of Hume's theories of sympathy and psychological causation we can excuse even the more wretched inhabitants of the *It's Always Sunny* universe. The McPoyles, Duncan and his violent drug gang, the bullies that tormented the Gang at school; we only see the worst of these people. Who knows what traumas twisted them into the assholes we see on the show? This cycle of misery will continue until we come to recognize and understand one another's faults and adopt a more compassionate way of rehabilitating one another, rather than punishing and avenging in a never-ending circle.

Of course we hate the Gang; they are detestable. Anyone that sets out to act like the members of the Gang is a jackass, and anyone that tries to claim their behavior is moral is just plain wrong. But we can recognize the faults of a house without blaming the house—we blame the builders.

The Gang were built and constructed by the world around them; copying greed here and developing resentment there with no positive sources of influence to set them right. They may be beyond saving, and we may never want them over for dinner, but we can rise above our natural instincts, be better than the Gang, and come to understand their flaws, to understand that we could have found ourselves with the same faults given the life they've had.

12
Ethics for Jabronis

SKYLER KING

No one wants to be a jabroni. Mac makes it clear that jabronis are complete losers. Every time Charlie says something remotely stupid, Mac always exclaims, "Don't be a jabroni, man!" And Charlie tries valiantly throughout the show to overcome his jabroniness. But what if each one of us happened to be a moral jabroni at one point in our lives? What if some of us *are* living in the totally uncool and lame position of jabroniness right now?

Now, obviously, your first reaction is probably, "Nah, Man. I'm a great person. I mean, look at me. I helped mow my neighbor's lawn last week and I go to church." While those may be commendable actions (although, it's unclear how going to church makes you any more or less morally decent than the next guy or gal), I think *It's Always Sunny* teaches us a very important lesson concerning the way we conduct our lives: namely, that we are often oblivious to a *massive* moral duty that slowly impugns our moral character and deadens our empathetic connectivity to others. And what moral duty might I be talking about here? Our moral obligations to those who suffer around and beyond us.

When it comes to addressing extreme suffering, many of us are like Dennis and Dee during the third episode of Season Three, "Dennis's and Dee's Mom Is Dead." As the title suggests, Dennis's and Dee's mom dies and the first thing Dennis and Dee do is start fighting over their mother's possessions. This "inheritance war" grows so extreme that Dennis and Dee actually start destroying several of their mother's possessions, just to keep the other sibling from acquiring them.

What does this scenario have to do with us and our moral duties? It's a potent metaphor for the difference between *greed* and *need*. Many of us probably pass beggars and homeless people every day on our way to work, school, the gym, or whatever else—but what are we doing to help these people? Perhaps some of us are acting out the scene between Dennis and Dee, but in a slightly different way: perhaps we are rushing to accumulate wealth, to horde fancy and shiny new material commodities to "display" our success, and being wrapped up solely in advancing our own lives that we forget about *the other*. All the while, while we chase the Almighty Dollar or a prestigious rank, we completly ignore the poor beggar, the despondent soul who walks our streets—the person who, as Charlie said of a homeless kid during his "cannibal scare," "No one in the world would possibly miss" ("Mac and Dennis: Manhunters"). Yet these "unmissable souls" are simply in need of a helping hand and a caring heart; many of them are dying unnoticed—and *we* might have been able to save them.

I believe that the enormous weight of the moral duty to help alleviate extreme suffering should scare us, should make us somewhat uncomfortable—should make us squirm like powerful sermons declaring the impending fire and brimstone, the imminent and eternal punishment of some jealous and angry deity. Why? Because this moral matter is that important. And, actually, *It's Always Sunny* subtly explores several possible responses we might give to the moral duty of helping those in extreme suffering.

But first, let's look at some of the reasons Dennis and Mac give for *not* helping those who suffer.

Poor People Suck, Man!

When I mentioned that we have a moral duty to help alleviate extreme suffering, some of you probably said what Dennis said: "Poor people? Why give all your money to poor people?" ("Charlie Gets Crippled"). Many people often feel that they work hard for their money and the poor person—the homeless person down the street—just sits on the street and never even tries to help himself. After all, what did Dennis and Dee do after they found out that they could go on welfare? They spent all their money on booze, a boom box, and sat around all day and all night drinking and jamming out to music ("Dennis and Dee Go On Welfare").

But did you know that many homeless and poor people are *not* like that? They're just like you and me: people who tried to work ridiculously hard to get ahead, but some tragic life circumstance—maybe a house fire; maybe the sudden death of a family member; maybe their employers downsized and laid-off half the employees—seemed to irreparably alter their lives.

Another reason people often give for ignoring the homeless or the downtrodden members of society is that there have been so many scams and generous people have been taken advantage of as a result. I don't know if I would call Dennis a very generous person, but he dropped everything to help Charlie when Charlie said he had cancer ("Charlie Has Cancer"). Even though Dennis *really* didn't want to help, he knew he couldn't let his bro down.

After all, what's a small inconvenience for someone who's about to croak? Really doesn't matter, right? Anyway, at the end of the episode, Charlie reveals that he *doesn't* have cancer. After hearing this, Dennis is so shocked and infuriated that he calls Charlie a bunch of naughty names and storms off, leaving Charlie all by himself. And that isn't the only time the Gang tries to help others only to get burned: Mac tries to help a Hispanic family get accustomed to the US, but the family doesn't understand English ("The Gang Gets Extreme: Makeover Home Edition"). As a result of this miscommunication, the family is terrified and—as a result of a prank pulled by Frank (that's some nice poetic skills, eh?)—Mac and Charlie end up destroying the family's new home. The family sues and gets a huge reward and

Mac complains, "Try to help people and you wind up getting screwed."

While I don't doubt that many people *have* been taken advantage of by scams, that doesn't mean that *all* poor people are scammers or that all relief efforts are just trying to take money from the poor saps dumb even to genuinely care about other human beings. After all, what does Bruce Mathis constantly try to tell us during the course of the show? He tells us that the needs of others—"others," here, defined as "those who are in extreme poverty; those who can't help themselves"—are more important than a Ferrari or a mansion or video games. Don't let the Dennises and Dees discourage you from making a real difference to those who are largely forgotten in the conscience of society.

It's Always Sunny provides us with *many* more examples of the "common mentality" towards the poor and oppressed that we could explore. But hopefully this is enough to satiate any immense worries or misgivings you might have harbored at the outset of this tantalizing chapter.

Charlie, Pass the Utility Knife

Perhaps the most famous and totally rad ethical system around today is *utilitarianism*. Utilitarianism can be defined in multiple ways, but the simplest definition is basically as follows: the right thing to do in any given circumstances is whatever will bring about the most good for the most people. Intuitively, Utilitarianism probably makes a lot of sense. To see why, just ponder the following scenario: Dennis walks down the block one morning, calmly drinking in the crisp Philly air, when he smells the repugnant smell of fire, brick, and alcohol. As he approaches Paddy's, he notices, much to his dismay, that the bar is one fire. At first, Dennis is dumbfounded. How could Paddy's catch on fire? While he contemplates what sort of stupid activities Charlie has been up to this time, he hears several screams from two directions: one from inside the burning Paddy's; and one from behind him. In a panic, Dennis paces back and forth and realizes that

Mac is trapped inside Paddy's; Charlie, Dee, and Frank are curled up in the fetal position in the middle of the street, trying to hide from a crazy axe murderer who is looming over them. So, who does Dennis save? Should he save his best friend Mac? Or Charlie, Dee, and Frank? From a Utilitarian perspective, the answer is, without question, that Dennis should save Charlie, Dee, and Frank.

That example might seem obvious or trivial, but let's consider what a recent philosopher named Peter Singer has to say about Utilitarianism. He provides a very formal representation of his central argument for why we should help those experience extreme suffering:

1. **If we can prevent something bad without sacrificing anything of comparable significance, we ought to do it.**

2. **Absolute poverty is bad.**

3. **There's some poverty we can prevent without sacrificing anything of comparable moral significance.**

4. **Therefore, we ought to prevent some absolute poverty.**

According to Singer's argument, if we aren't *actively* helping or trying to prevent extreme suffering, then we're failing to perform our moral duties; if we're failing to perform our moral duties, then we're not moral people. So, on Singer's view, charity isn't a "nice thing" to do—it's a *requirement*.

Singer's argument has further implications, though. His argument means that whether or not Dennis should buy a new car depends on the following considerations (and many others): a. whether or not Dennis can get by with his current car; b. whether the money Dennis is taking out of his account to purchase this new car will make more of a difference when donated than the (possibly) minimal improvement of a "luxury" car for him; and c. whether Dennis really *needs* that car.

137

Now, we might be tempted to say that the Gang is exempt from Singer's argument because they are pretty poor too and they are struggling business owners. However, Singer would probably say something like, "They are not *trying* to work. The Gang's quasi-suffering is self-imposed whereas many who are living in abject poverty did *not* choose those conditions."

Out of the diverse cast on the show, probably the only character who consistently and truthfully adheres to the Utilitarian creed is Bruce Mathis. He spends a lot of time trying to cheer up children in hospitals and helping children overseas ("Dennis and Dee Get a New Dad"); he donates the small fortune he inherited from his estranged wife to help a local and downtrodden Muslim organization ("The Gang Solves the Gas Crisis"); and he also donates part of his salary to various charities.

So, if we subscribe to Singer's Utilitarianism, then we'd better donate a considerable amount of our time or energy to helping those who are less fortunate than ourselves—otherwise, as Singer argues, we are *failing* to be *morally good* people. If this doesn't sound tractable to you, then perhaps you shouldn't ask Charlie to pass you the utility knife.

Nodding Towards Caring

Perhaps you, like the Gang, didn't really like Singer's approach to morality. Maybe you want to find another moral philosopher to ask about our obligations to the less fortunate. Maybe you're cool with giving, but you don't want it to be a requirement. Well, another philosopher, named Nel Noddings, developed what she called "a feminist approach to ethics." Her motto for this new ethical system is "caring." And, if you didn't like Singer's system, you will be happy to know that Noddings's "caring" conflicts with Singer's Utilitarian approach—somewhat.

Noddings's fundamental idea was that we're only obligated to help those around us because they are "within our reach" and we can "see the completion of our actions in the other." By "completion in the other," Noddings seems to mean that we can observe the difference our actions make. So, if you live in Boston, Massachusetts, you're only required to help the less fortunate in Boston; if you live in Collins, Missouri, then you're only required to help the people in Collins. *But* we could restrict our "range of obligation" even further than that, if we wanted. Since Boston is a huge city, it might seem unfair that Bostonians have a heavier moral burden than the residents of the small town of Collins, Missouri. So, in order to make things more "fair," we might say that Bostonians only have to help the people in their individual neighborhoods. If we reduce our "range of obligation" like this, then perhaps the Bostonians won't have to do more work to obtain "moral goodness" than the people of Collins.

Moreover, Noddings would say that Ben Mathis does not need to spend so much time helping children overseas—he *can* if he wants to, but he is under no *obligation* to help those children. So, what's a good example of "morally obligated" assistance that Noddings would deem appropriate? Well, remember when Frank sold Charlie's apartment and then Mac and Dennis fired Charlie ("The Great Recession")? Charlie asked if he could either sleep in the bar or stay with Dennis and Mac, but Dennis and Mac swiftly denied him access to either the bar or their apartment. Then, the following conversation occurred:

CHARLIE: Where am I supposed to live?

MAC: [*condescendingly*] It's the recession. Times are tough. You'll bounce back.

DENNIS: [*d-bag like*] We're not in the business of giving hand-outs, Charlie. We're not the government.

According to Noddings's view, Dennis and Mac *should* have helped Charlie. After all, Charlie lives in their neighborhood, they could have observed their action being *completed* in the other (that is, they could have seen the good their actions brought about for Charlie), and, most importantly, Charlie is their main man—their homie. Following Noddings's approach, Mac and Dennis totally bombed upholding their moral duties. They should have nodded towards caring and "helped a brotha out."

Dee's Objection to Noddings's "Caring"

Presumably, Mac and Dennis don't like someone else telling them how to live their lives. So, being the semi-juveniles that they are, they need to search for a way to get out of Noddings's ethical ruling. Our objection to Singer was that he required *a lot* from us in order to be considered morally good people. But can we find some way to help Mac and Dennis out of their moral dilemma?

One objection people have raised to Noddings's system is that it doesn't really seem like we *care*. We have to help the Charlies in our neighborhood after we fire them from their jobs, but we don't have to do anything about people who are suffering elsewhere in our state or our country—or even our *world*? If that's the moral requirement for a system supposedly based on "caring," then it seems like our capacity for caring is extremely limited. According to Noddings's theory, we seem like the police officer lady who grew aggravated when Charlie burst in claiming to have proof of corrupt local police and politicians ("Bums Making a Mess All Over the City"). After Charlie leaves, the police officer lady says, "Man, we have *got* to do something about those homeless people." In other words, Noddings's view seems to allow us to view those who are less fortunate than us as *problems* or *inconveniences*. We seem to be required to care only when someone else's misfortunate might have a direct impact upon us. But what about all the other people who need help—like in Africa? It doesn't seem like those people's local community can do much to help them. So, we're just supposed to *not* care about those people?

Another objection people have raised to Noddings's theory is that it seems awfully selfish for something that is ostensibly about "caring." Remember how Dennis and Mac were required to help Charlie, according to Noddings, because they could see the good that their action brought about? (Or, to use Noddings' terminology, they could see "the completion in the other.") Some people think it doesn't matter whether or not we can "see the good" our actions bring about; what matters is that there is a tremendous need in the world and many people *can't* help themselves. So, some think, we need to help as many people as we can, regardless of whether we ever know if we're making a difference. Our humanitarian efforts shouldn't be about *us*, but about genuinely trying to help others.

If we fail to help others because we can't see the good it does, then we seem like Dennis, Mac, and Charlie when Dee was pregnant ("Who Got Dee Pregnant?"): the most attention they paid to her was when she first told them she was pregnant. The Gang, minus Dee, sat around recalling their last Halloween party and tried to remember if any of them had accidentally had sex with Dee. Turns out, none of them did. So, the Gang forgot about it.

After that night, the guys didn't really care about Dee's pregnancy much. In fact, Dennis always made fun of her for eating a lot and complained about her "neediness." Mack and Charlie were similar stories. The only time the guys did care was when Dee suddenly blurted out, "One of you is the father!" ("Dee Gives Birth") At that point, the guys immediately grow concerned about Dee and the baby—they became *obsessively* concerned about it. But when Dee told Dennis, Mac, and Charlie that she was just kidding about them being the father, the guys all ran off, explicitly saying they didn't care about Dee or her baby. In other words, Dee's pregnancy was an inconvenience to the guys until they thought *they* were responsible for her pregnancy. And, if we take Noddings's view, then we seem to only care about others when others' needs potentially inconvenience us. So, it seems that Dee would have a major gripe accepting Noddings's "caring" system.

Is It Always Sunny in *Your* Philadelphia?

There are many other approaches to ethics—and, specifically, the problem of extreme suffering—that we could look at, but we have examined a couple of likely positions—Singer and Noddings.

The blanket framing of Singer's Utilitarianism—that is, the "the greatest good" must be manifested—sounds like an amazing thing to say, but it is much harder to live by. Noddings's approach sounds like something you will often hear more conservative people say ("Why don't I just help those people around me and let someone else take care of all the other people in the world? I'm not responsible for people across the world!"); however, some of the motivations for her "caring" approach seem ribald due to the somewhat selfish nature of her limits on "caring."

Regardless of the differences and diversities of opinion in moral philosophy, I think most philosophers would agree that we should do *something* to help those who are much less fortunate than we are. Even the Gang seems to subconsciously grasp this truth at times: sometimes they are forced to help others ("The Gang Gives Back"); other times they try to help, but end up creating a disaster ("The Gang Gets Extreme: Makeover Home Edition"); and other times they genuinely believe they are doing something helpful for others, like intervening when Frank seems to have "lost his marbles" ("The Gang Gives Frank an Intervention").

If Mac were here, he would probably pull out his *Bible* and start quoting scriptures to convince you to help others. But here's another reason: a significant portion of the world's population is living in extreme suffering. Some estimates rank fifty percent of the population under that umbrella. Yet we often worry about whether our car looks "nice" or that our TV is only a thirty-inch flat screen and not a seventy-inch one; we complain (perhaps every morning) that the line at Starbucks is taking too long—but all the while hundreds and hundreds, even thousands, of people are dying because they couldn't get enough to eat last night or because their drinking water is so sickeningly polluted that they can't drink it.

What I'm saying is this: it's all a matter of perspective. For most mid- to upper-middle class Americans, live is just grand; our complaints are really nit-picking. Unfortunately, though, there are many children all over the world who wish they could throw away a hamburger from McDonald's just because it didn't taste too good.

So, what I'm asking is this: please consider how much time and money you spend on frivolous things. I'm not going as far as Singer and arguing that you should live in the "margins"—that is, not have any more than you absolutely need. However, I am asking that you consider donating to Oxfam or UNICEF or some other respectable charity; I am asking that you consider spending a Saturday morning volunteering at Convoy of Hope or a soup kitchen or coaching a Youth's League basketball game like Dennis and Dee ("The Gang Gives Back"); I am asking that you consider the starving child in New York City or Africa or, perhaps, *in your own town* before you send a half-eaten plate back with the waiter or waitress at a restaurant; I am asking that you pause, just for a few moments, before you buy something "just because" and consider how you might potentially make a positive difference in the world if you were to spend a little less on toys and invest a little in *saving a life.*

In America, we have the luxury of talking about the poor in spirit; but what are we doing to uplift the spirit of the poor? We complain about someone having a poor outlook on life; but what are we doing to brighten the outlook of and *on* the poor? We can complain that our country might eventually go financially bankrupt; but do we realize that each of us, individually, will quickly go *morally* bankrupt without *actively* helping those who are less fortunate than ourselves?

If any of the characters in *It's Always Sunny* provide a good model for us to follow, I think it's Ben Mathis. He seems to genuinely care and he isn't afraid to go out of his way to help those who can't help themselves—and even those who *can* help themselves, but need a boost to get going on the right track. But let's not discount the positive examples that each member of the Gang provides for us to consider: Dennis joins a protest to stand up for environmentalist concerns while Dee and Mac decide to rescue and raise a dumpster baby ("The Gang Finds a Dumpster Baby"); the Gang tries to change the political structure of Philly ("The Gang Runs for Office); and Frank tries to hire workers from the welfare system ("Dennis and Dee Go On Welfare"). Even though the Gang always allows their greed to overcome the need in front of them, they still try to help numerous times—and *that* is something from which we can learn.

In the end, it matters not what you have, but what you have done. So, I ask you: is it always sunny in *your* Philadelphia?

V

Truth

13
The Gang's Crooked Thinking

FENNER TANSWELL

MAC: You said that word `implication' a few times. . . . What
implication?

—"The Gang Buys a Boat"

Move aside, moral philosophy! It's pretty clear that the gang
are immoral, but what I'm going to tell you about is that they
are also entirely *illogical*.

You can use Logic in math, it's vital for programming
computers and you can apply it to analyzing languages.
Right now, though, we'll think about how it's used in *reasoning*. In this sense, Logic is all about what follows from what.

Another way of putting this is, given some facts or pieces
of information, what you can figure out for certain from
them. We call the starting facts the *premises*, the things you
figure out the *conclusions* and the process of going from one
to the other an *argument*. Here are some arguments:

- **If poop is funny, then Frank pooped in the bed.**
- **Poop is funny.**

- **Frank pooped in the bed.**

And

- Dennis uses the D.E.N.N.I.S. system.
- If Dennis uses the D.E.N.N.I.S. system, then he will get laid.
- If Dennis gets laid, then Dennis will videotape it.
- If Dennis videotapes it, Mac will watch the video of Dennis getting laid.

- **Mac will watch the video of Dennis getting laid.**

Both of these arguments are *valid*. That means that the conclusion follows from the premises entirely because of structure of the argument itself.

In Logic, we say that the premises together *imply* the conclusion.

It doesn't really matter what the premises and conclusion *say* for an argument to be valid, instead what is important is the shape, or *form*, of the argument. For example, the following argument has exactly the same form as the first one we saw:

- **If Sweet Dee looks like a bird, then the rest of the gang will make fun of her.**
- **Sweet Dee looks like a bird.**

- **The rest of the Gang will make fun of her.**

This form of argument is called *Modus Ponens*. When I say that what's important is having the right form, it might sound a bit vague and uncertain, but one of the first things you do in Logic is to make this precise. Let's not bother with that here, but it's not so tricky if you want to go away and find out!

Here's a question, though: if it's the form of an argument that's important and what the sentences actually say isn't, what about when they say something false? Let's see another case of Modus Ponens where one of the premises is false:

- **If the McPoyles are sexy, then the Gang will like having them at Paddy's.**
- **The McPoyles are sexy.**

- **The Gang will like having them at Paddy's.**

I hope you agree that the second premise here is false. What has happened, though, is that the conclusion is also false, because the gang really hates having the McPoyles at Paddy's. Saying that, the argument is of the right form (still Modus Ponens!) so it is still definitely valid by what we have said before. But, don't worry, this does make sense: the conclusion does seem to follow from the premises. So what's going on? The difference in this case was that the argument wasn't *sound*.

We say, in Logic, that an argument is sound if (and only if!) it is valid plus it has all true premises. The brilliant thing is that if you start with true premises and have a valid argument form, then you will guarantee that your conclusion is also true *with absolute certainty*! In the argument about the McPoyles, we had a valid form but we did not have true premises, so the argument wasn't sound, and so it didn't guarantee us a true conclusion!

Isn't Logic fun? Not only that, but it's really useful for reasoning in the real world. We constantly need to use knowledge we have to figure out more things. With Logic, this will all go swimmingly.

However, without Logic to guide you, you can easily and very quickly run into all sorts of problems where reasoning goes wrong and leads you astray. This happens to the Gang almost constantly, so I will run through a few different arguments that appear in the show, particularly in "Reynolds vs. Reynolds: The Cereal Defense," and see how obvious fallacies that they fall into to illustrate just how bad it is when reasoning goes awry.

Disclaimer: once you are aware of what kinds of arguments are fallacious, you will see them everywhere: in ads, from politicians, from friends, and from family. The author wishes in no way to be responsible for any arguments, fallings-out, changes of beliefs or changes of political affiliation caused by your new-found ability to spot mistakes in Logic!

On Donkey-Brains

In "Reynolds vs Reynolds: The Cereal Defense" the Gang's trying to settle the matter of who should pay for damages to Dennis's car. On the one hand, Frank crashed into the back of him because he couldn't see properly (Frank says "I can see. I got glasses. I just need new lenses"), but on the other hand Dennis was eating cereal behind the wheel of his car. Having set up their courtroom, the Gang begin the trial with an argument from Charlie for Frank concerning donkey-brains:

> **DENNIS:** Donkey-brained?
>
> **CHARLIE:** It means to have the brains of a donkey or donkey-like creature.
>
> **DENNIS:** Okay, I think I know what it means, but if anything it's not donkey-brained to drive around with a bowl of cereal. It is donkey-brained to drive around without the use of your vision.
>
> **CHARLIE:** Oh, that's interesting. So you do admit that someone who makes foolish decisions could be considered donkey-brained?
>
> **DENNIS:** Er, sure, yeah, okay, fine.

It then turns out that Frank has an official certificate which declares that he does not have donkey-brains! Charlie goes on:

> **CHARLIE:** Well, Dennis, if by your own admission someone who has donkey-brains could be considered reckless or moronic or idiotic and my client Frank here has a state-issued certificate clearing him of having said donkey-brains then I ask you this: do you have any such certificate?

That Dennis doesn't have a similar certificate is enough for the rest of the Gang to swing towards Frank's side on Mac's Trial Meter.

So what's going on here? Part of it seems to be this argument:

- **If someone makes foolish decisions, then they are donkey-brained.**
- **Frank is not donkey-brained.**

- **Frank does not make foolish decisions.**

This argument form is called *Modus Tollens* and is valid according to classical logic (which is the standard go-to set of logical rules), so if the premises are true and the argument is thus sound, then it has been shown through the argument that Frank could not have been making a foolish decision to drive around without being able to see. Of course, we have seen that if a conclusion to a valid argument seems fishy, we should look back at the premises to see if any of them are false.

Let's have a look at both of them to see what the problems might be.

It seems that the first premise might be false because we can make some foolish decisions without being donkey-brained. The passage quoted above has Charlie trying very hard to establish this premise and Dennis reluctantly granting it because he is not aware of the trap that is about to be sprung. The second premise, that Frank is not donkey-brained, is supported entirely by the certificate that Frank has from when he was a child.

The Gang fully accept the certificate as definite proof that Frank is not donkey-brained, but how genuinely reliable it might be is still up for grabs. Either way, though, the problems we might have with this piece of reasoning is not about validity but about soundness. We appreciate that the argument has a valid form, but we suspect that the premises might be false.

However, the other part of what's going on in this argument is the question of whether Dennis is donkey-brained. Suppose the argument is something like this:

- **Dennis can't prove he isn't donkey-brained**
- **If Dennis is donkey-brained, then he was the one being reckless.**

- **Dennis was the one being reckless.**

This argument doesn't have a valid form. The fallacy here is the step from not being able to prove something is false to its being true. Taking something to be true because it hasn't been proven to be false is known as an *argument from ignorance*, and this type of argument is wrong—it's a fallacy. One common way of explaining why this is a fallacy is to say that not having evidence for something does not automatically count as evidence against it.

In this scene, Dennis rightly brings up the *burden of proof*. In argumentation, the burden of proof rests with the person who's trying to claim or assert something to be the case. In this case the burden of proof rests with Charlie to show that Dennis is donkey-brained. But the lack of a certificate that Dennis is not donkey-brained does not provide any evidence that he is.

In other cases, for example when in the same episode Mac claims that he could produce mutated offspring who could bend steel, the burden of proof is on Mac. When you have the burden of proof, it's up to you to give evidence for your position and failing to give any can count against you. Knowing where the burden of proof lies is a vital skill for anyone wanting to argue properly and be aware when others don't.

A neat example of this comes earlier in the episode when the Gang are deciding who the defendant in the case they are building should be. Dee utters one of my favorite lines:

DEE: He's right. Whenever someone is accused of something I automatically assume they are guilty.

So it turns out that Dee doesn't have a good grasp of burden of proof at all!

Mac's Credibility as a Witness

It emerges over the course of the trial that Mac seems to have a lot of sway in the Gang, especially over Charlie who will be one of the deciding votes as to who pays for the damages to Dennis's car. Dee tries to undermine this by attacking Mac's credibility, pointing to his bizarre beliefs that he can produce a super-race from his seed by genetic mutation and evolution. Dee says:

> **DEE:** If your character isn't credible, then are your arguments?

Then later:

> **DEE:** If you believe something that insane, how can you be our taste-maker? How can we believe anything you say?

Dee's tactic in her argument here is one of the best-known fallacies of all: attacking the advocate, or the *ad hominem* fallacy. The problem is arguing against the person that is making arguments and claims, rather than against the truth or validity of the claims themselves. While it may be the case that their character is untrustworthy, when it comes to arguments and reasoning it's not sufficient to undermine the credibility of the person, for their arguments might still be sound. Outside of Logic, showing that someone isn't credible is used all the time as a way of winning arguments (just think of smear tactics in politics). From a logical point of view, it's very important not to fall into the trap of thinking an argument doesn't work just because you know negative things about the person presenting it.

Science Is a Liar Sometimes

To further continue the ad hominem assassination of Mac's credibility, Dennis gets Mac to elaborate on his view that

153

evolution is "bullshit." Mac happily embraces the opportunity to wax lyrical about his views on this matter, and in the process produces a whole hotbed of logical fallacies. He starts like this:

> Mac: I'm not going to stand here and present some egg-head scientific argument based on fact. I'm just a regular dude. I like to drink beer, y'know, I love my family. Rock, flag, and eagle, right, Charlie? . . . I won't change my mind, because I don't have to, because I'm an American. I won't change my mind on anything, regardless of the facts set out before me. I'm dug in, and I'll never change.

Part of the problem with this is the dismissal of science based on its being too detached from the regular dudes. Logic and reasoning are equally valid for everybody and liking beer does not make you immune (at least, I really hope not)! Additionally, Mac makes it sound as if listening to any kind of scientific arguments is unpatriotic. This is clearly not the kind of argumentative move that could be supported by any good logic. Finally, the joke of the whole piece is that he is explicit in refusing to be swayed by any kind of arguments. Logic help us!

Dennis's reply to Mac's speech is this:

> Dennis: Mac, you're not going to get us to not believe in evolution. . . . The smartest scientists in all the world agree it is real.

What Dennis is doing here is an *appeal to authority*, another well-known fallacy. The fallacy is to just point to someone who knows more about your subject and say that because they believe it, it must be true. The problem is that even smart and knowledgeable people sometimes believe crazy and stupid things. Just look at philosophers; we can barely agree on anything, even when we know a lot about it. The point is, the beliefs of whichever person you are pointing to should be backed up with evidence and sound reasoning, so saying that they believe it is not enough by itself.

Mac rightly doesn't accept the appeal to authority that Dennis makes, but his response is amusingly just as bad: he reveals a poster he has made entitled "Science Is a Liar Sometimes." On it he has the faces of three people who were the smartest scientists in the entire world during their lives (Sir Isaac Newton, in particular, "blows everybody's nips off with his big brains"). By showing that Aristotle, Galileo, and Newton all held beliefs which turned out to be false, Mac declares that they made themselves and everybody on Earth look "like a bitch."

This kind of argument certainly stands against the appeal to authority, since it shows that people who are authorities on things still don't have to get everything right, but we had already seen that that kind of argument was fallacious anyway. We had also already seen that calling someone a bitch like Mac does is attacking the advocate, and so also not acceptable as good argumentation.

There are extra fallacies going on in what Mac is saying, though. He isn't just trying to refute the one appeal to authority by Dennis; he is trying to attack the credibility of science in general! By showing that great scientists of the past also got things wrong, Mac wants to suggest that our modern scientists might be wrong too, so evolution could be wrong. The fallacy here is known as a *straw man*. A straw man is used when you present the position you are arguing against as claiming something that they don't, where this extra claim is the "straw man" which is something easier to argue against (known as a straw man because straw men are much easier to blow over, not offering the resistance of real people and arguments).

In this case, Mac is wrong to present the scientific method as claiming to be infallible. Really, the whole point is following the evidence and choosing the best explanation for observed phenomena, which might change as new evidence becomes available (and as did happen from Aristotle to Newton, via Galileo). That the greatest scientific minds never get things wrong is a straw man that is much easier to refute by argument than an actual position anyone would hold.

However, Mac is also guilty of what is called *equivocation*. Using his bitch argument, he intends to show that there is reasonable doubt concerning evolution. Equivocation is when a single word is used to mean two different things, and using that confusing ambiguity an argument which is invalid can be snuck through. In this case, the kind of doubt that is obtained from the fact that the greatest scientists are never infallible is not the same as the kind of doubt as in the phrase "reasonable doubt." We may understand this in terms of burden of proof, as we saw described earlier.

The first kind of doubt is just about the mere possibility that something could go wrong: there is solid evidence, but we have historical precedent that sometimes scientific revolutions overturn this and skeptical worries, like those found in René Descartes's work, about the possibility of knowing anything for certain at all. Nonetheless, depending on the details, there may be good reasons to feel confident that this won't happen. In the case of reasonable doubt, there is simply not enough evidence to support the conclusion in the first place. The theory of evolution is beyond reasonable doubt, but not immune to the more skeptical version of doubt. Mac has spoken about skeptical doubt and equivocated it with reasonable doubt!

Go Forth and Use Logic

In the end, the Gang decides that Dee has to pay for the damages to both cars, for comedy rather than on any logical basis.

What we have seen is why Logic is useful in identifying good reasoning and where arguments can go wrong. The set-up to many episodes of *It's Always Sunny* is that the Gang disagree on some issue and so go off to investigate both sides. Keep an eye out in future for the way that the arguments are structured and how hilarious it is when the gang use obviously incorrect arguments.

My advice, then, is to go forth and use Logic! Every day people try to convince you of things using arguments. The more Logic you know, the better you'll be able to tell when they are leading you astray!

MAC: Okay, that was the implication, right?

DENNIS: That was definitely the implication! ("The Gang Buys a Boat")

14
Why Science Is a Liar Sometimes

Russ Hamer

Though we would never consider the Gang to be scientists, they actually follow the scientific method quite often. When Dennis has a theory about how to attract women, he tests that theory by invoking the D.E.N.N.I.S. system. I think that we can safely assume that this system did not come to Dennis as divine inspiration, but rather that he developed it over years of trial and error.

While they might be idiots, the Gang generally employs the scientific method in working through their schemes. They start with a hypothesis and endeavor to test it, ultimately coming to a conclusion as to whether it was a good or bad hypothesis based on their test results. When Mac's character is attacked in "Reynolds vs Reynolds: The Cereal Defense" he puts science on trial. He's able to successfully make the Gang doubt the theory of evolution by showing that every scientist in the past is a bitch, and no one wants to look like a bitch.

The Cereal Defense

The episode begins with Frank running into Dennis's car because Frank is mostly blind. Dennis had been eating a bowl of cereal while driving, and thus when he was hit, the cereal spilled everywhere, causing damage to the interior of his car. Dennis wants Frank to pay for the damage, but Frank thinks that Dennis is at fault because it's irresponsible to eat cereal while driving. The gang decides to settle the matter internally, and a trial is held, with both Dennis and Frank declaring themselves to be the defendant. Charlie is mostly swayed by Mac's decision on who the guilty party is and Mac is leaning towards giving Frank the victory. Thus, Dee, who is on Dennis's side, decides to attack Mac's credibility by making him explain that he doesn't believe in evolution. It's at this point where our issue arises.

Mac defends his beliefs by showing that many scientists in the past have been wrong. He goes through Aristotle, Galileo, and finally Newton to show that each man proved wrong the previous man, making him look like a bitch. Mac's point is that each scientist was eventually proven wrong, and therefore science can't be trusted. Dennis's reply is that Mac is basing his belief set on a bunch of words in a book written by people that he has never met, whereas evolution is supported by verified data and fossil records. Mac responds by asking Dennis whether or not he has seen this data or these fossil records. When Dennis admits that he hasn't, Mac claims that Dennis must then only believe in evolution based on a kind of faith, since both of them are reading books written by people that they don't know, and are basing their beliefs on those books.

This claim is enough to throw everyone into doubt about whether or not evolution is real. What Mac has successfully done is convince the gang that believing in evolution requires just as much faith as believing in God, and thus that both beliefs are equally justifiable. The question for us is, how do we separate a scientific belief from a religious one?

Dennis Is Asshole, Why Charlie Hate?

A number of philosophers have put forward arguments that define certain theories as scientific. Chief among them is Karl Popper and his falsification thesis. Popper claims that scientific theories start with specific bits of data, and we form theories based on those bits of data. For instance, looking at the fact that Charlie and Mac have never won a game of CharDee MacDennis might lead you to conclude that they are not very good at CharDee MacDennis.

Popper argues that all science happens according to this kind of process. There's some evidence for just about any claim. How, then, are we to judge the strength of particular claims? Charlie ignores every instance of the waitress being mean to him and only remembers instances of her being nice. So Charlie has a number of data points that lead him to believe that he and the waitress will one day be together. He makes a general claim, or theory, based on the evidence that he recognizes. Unfortunately, Charlie is only looking at some of the evidence. He is picking the data that he wants, and making generalizations based on that incomplete data.

These are what are known as confirming instances. As has been shown, the problem with confirming instances is that we can find them for any theory whatsoever. Most pseudoscience is based on confirming instances. When you look at something like astrology, most of the predictions that are made are vague. The more vague a prediction, the less of a risk that prediction takes. If I tell you that tomorrow at noon, someone will stab you, I am making a precise prediction, and it would be quite remarkable if that prediction were to be confirmed. If, on the other hand, I tell you that in the next month you will experience a moment of pain, neither the precise time nor the cause of the pain have been specified, so the prediction is pretty safe.

For this reason Popper claims that confirming instances should only be considered decisive if they come about from a risky prediction. If I make a risky prediction, a prediction that makes a precise claim that you might not expect to occur, then if my prediction comes true, my theory that gave rise to that prediction has passed a strong test, and might be true. When Einsteinian special relativity came about, it made a number of risky predictions, predictions that according to the then-current understanding of physics, should not happen. Thus when those events did happen, like the deflection of light by the Sun's mass, they counted as strong confirmations of Einstein's theory.

And so Popper argues that the real differentiation between a scientific and a non-scientific theory is falsifiability. A scientific theory says that if some specific event happens, the theory will have been falsified. A scientific theory therefore takes a big risk. By contrast, non-scientific predictions, like those of astrology, take very little risk, because they are usually so vague they are likely to be confirmed by chance.

When Mac is defending his character, he makes the claim, "I won't change my mind, 'cause I don't have to, 'cause I'm an American. I won't change my mind on anything, regardless of the facts that are set out before me. I'm dug in, and I'll never change." This is precisely what typifies the non-scientific approach. Mac is describing his views as being un-falsifiable. Regardless of any amount of fact or evidence, Mac will never admit that he was wrong, and thus his beliefs are not scientific. A scientific belief must always admit of the possibility of falsification.

If we look at another episode, "The Gang Solves the Gas Crisis," we see a case where the scientific method is embraced by the Gang. Numerous times, when the plan fails, the Gang realizes that their theory didn't work, and they try to adjust accordingly. Mac being the brains and the muscle didn't work, and they moved away from that theory as soon as it was falsified. None of their group configurations worked (likely because Charlie doesn't really know how to be a wild card), but each time a group configuration failed, the group adjusted their theory, and went ahead to test their new theory. With this approach, we can certainly see how there is a distinct difference between Mac's righteous belief in the saints who wrote the Bible, and Dennis's donkey-brained belief in evolution.

Seeing Is Believing

This brings us to our next point: it's okay to be a science bitch. Mac doesn't want to accept the claims of scientists, because historically, scientific theories have all been proven wrong. Since past scientists have been proven wrong, why should we trust current scientists? Even if we can distinguish Mac's belief as being nonscientific, and Dennis's belief as being scientific (assuming that he believes in evolution because it's a good theory), that doesn't seem to help in explaining why we should accept scientific claims.

Here, we can turn to another philosopher, Thomas Kuhn. Kuhn distinguishes between two different kinds of science, normal science and revolutionary science. Normal science is what happens most of the time. When the Gang is trying to figure out which group configuration works best so that they can solve the gas crisis, they are doing normal science. There is an overarching assumption that getting the correct configuration will solve their problems. So even when they run into a falsifying instance, they don't view it as problematic overall. Instead, it is only problematic for one specific facet of their overall theory.

Kuhn calls these overarching assumptions "paradigms." Most of the time, scientists work within a specific paradigm. They are all working under the same basic assumptions, which are that they just need to fine tune their roles in the group, and everything will run smoothly. Given that paradigm, the falsifications don't falsify the paradigm, but only one small theory within the paradigm, or one interpretation of it.

So when we work under the same paradigm, falsification doesn't actually falsify the whole theory. If I'm a Newtonian physicist and I run an experiment that shows that time and space are interrelated, no one would assume that Newtonian physics must be wrong. Instead, they would claim that I made an error, or that Newtonian physics can account for the phenomenon that I have observed. When we do normal science, we're not questioning our paradigm, so when we run into falsifications, we find some way to explain them away, or to make an adjustment to the theory.

But sometimes, says Kuhn, normal science gives way to revolutionary science. Over time, more and more problems pile up so that some people begin to suspect a radically different approach may be called for. Newtonian physics suddenly found it had a serious problem on its hands, because Einstein's paradigm seemed to explain the universe better than Newton's. When confronted with this conflict, we enter into revolutionary science.

Rock, Flag, and Eagle

In his attempt to discredit modern science, Mac recognizes the historical shifts in the world view of scientists, but where Popper seems to find confidence, Mac finds distrust. Why trust the findings of people who are constantly wrong? As we have seen, this is precisely how science operates. Science works by disproving past assumptions, and coming up with better ones. But the real question is whether this should make us abandon science. Mac seems to think that it should. But why should we consider it a weakness in science that it is always ready to revise its conclusions? Wht not instead consider that a strength?

In "The Gang Exploits a Miracle" the Gang finds a water stain in the bar's office, and Mac claims that it's a stain of the Virgin Mary. The rest of the Gang are very skeptical, claiming that it's most likely just a water stain caused by leaky pipes. Mac, however, insists that it's a miracle, or a divine sign.

In this situation, Mac is unwilling to change his mind. Even when the church refuses to recognize the stain as a miracle, Mac takes it to be a sign that he should become a minister. Yet, he quickly fails at that pursuit. Though his theory regarding the miracle seems to have been falsified, Mac does not accept that as having happened. Just as when he said that he was "dug in" during the cereal defense, Mac seems to be "dug in" in regarding all of his religious beliefs. He has a belief set about morals and religion and nothing that anyone says or does will ever change that. Should we not recognize this as a weakness in his beliefs?

If it's a weakness that Mac's beliefs will never change, then revise-ability seems to be a strength. This is precisely what the scientific approach offers. Though Mac wants us to be skeptical about scientific claims, his approach seems to be one that is based entirely on personal pride. I don't think that this should surprise us at all. It's not as if the Gang is intellectually rigorous, or really, anything more than petty. Mac recognizes that sometimes scientists are wrong, and so he tries to scare everyone else into fearing that they might be wrong. This is the same kind of logic that would drive someone to say, "If I have no expectations, then I'm never disappointed." But that doesn't make expectations bad, it just makes you a coward. So to with the gang and their views about science. Science being wrong sometimes doesn't make science bad, it is in fact precisely its ability to correct itself that makes it good. So to lack belief in scientific claims just because science is sometimes wrong doesn't help us avoid looking like a science bitch, it instead just makes us look like a bitch.

Reasonable Doubt

Popper and Kuhn would both agree however, that science is not aimed at finding ultimate truth, but rather at giving the most accurate description of the universe that is possible, given the information we have. Mac seems to be concerned with attaining some kind of ultimate truth, and thus since science has been wrong in the past, it must not lead us towards the ultimate truth. Mac is missing the point here. Science isn't trying to lead us towards ultimate truth. Instead, science is primarily concerned with providing us with the best possible description of the universe in which we live.

We shouldn't believe in evolution based on the idea that evolution has been proven to be absolutely true. No scientific theory can ever provide us with such assurance. Instead, we should believe in evolution because it's currently the best theory we have for describing the evidence that we find in nature. Because it provides us with a very accurate description and explanation of all the relevant facts, evolution is a good theory and one worth putting our trust in.

If what Mac really wants is absolute truth, then he will never find it in science. In order for a theory to be scientific, that theory has to be potentially disprovable. Maybe Mac is correct in asserting that evolution isn't real. And maybe in the future some bright group of scientists will present a theory that better accounts for the facts. As good scientists, we should look forward to that day, and welcome it with open arms.

If that happens though, Mac will have been right for all the wrong reasons. We shouldn't be afraid of looking like a science bitch; instead we should revel in scientific progress.

15
The Gang Solves the Gas Crisis as a Nietzschean Parable

MARTYN JONES

Friedrich Nietzsche (1844–1900) sits in a massive rocking chair. He's frowning out the window at a bare branch as it bobs in the rain. Three boys are playing in this room, which is a large study. There's a fire going in the hearth. It seems downright idyllic, except that Nietzsche is pissed.

"Will you kids be quiet?" he says.

They laugh and run to the far side of the room.

"Ha-ha, Uncle Fred! You can't get us over here. Why don't we stay right here until we grow old and you are dead and the world has become perfect?" a boy named Mac says.

The boys chuckle.

"A perfect world, eh? What kind of nonsense is this?" says Nietzsche toward the window.

"Ja, Uncle Fred!" Dennis calls from across the room, "the world is becoming better, and not only that, but our understanding of it! Soon we will have everything mapped out—not only places, but true ideas. And even the ideas of the ideas!"

Dennis throws his head back like a bird and laughs, and as he laughs the others throw back their heads and start to laugh along with it. They are in a laughing sort of mood.

"What foolishness," Nietzsche says to himself. "Really, what a bunch of idiots."

At this point a foam football arcs over from the far side of the room and beans him in the temple.

"What foolishness! What idiots! Which one of you did that?"

The boys laugh.

"Come over here and sit at my feet right this minute!"

Still chuckling, the boys nonetheless make a meandering path over to Uncle Fred. Charlie, the third boy, lags behind a little bit. He is also glancing out the window.

"Okay, you idiots, it's story time. I'm going to show you why your ideas about reality and the world are baseless and will lead to destruction."

"Stories are a waste of time!"

"Shut up, you idiot, Mac! Stupid!"

"Hah hah."

"Okay, now listen, you idiots. This is a story about you. It happens in the future, which is something I actually know a hell of a lot about."

"Yeah, right!"

"Shut up, Dennis! You are worse than Mac."

"Hah hah . . . um, you don't mean that, do you?"

"Anyways, as I was saying, this is a story about you three in the future. First off, you are all Americans."

There are cries of protest from all three boys.

"Yes, you are all Americans, and you are also drunken idiots, but that last part is certainly no revelation."

Again, cries of protest.

"Seriously, kids, listen to me or the next century is going to be very difficult for you."

The boys quiet down but continue to fidget.

"Okay then. The three of you live in America, and you own a bar together. You know, a pub. A beer garden, sort of."

The boys cheer.

"Shut up. Okay, so, in the future, people get places using cars, which are like trains except they don't run on rails. Or they're like carriages, but they don't have horses. And to operate, they burn gasoline in their engines, which turns the wheels."

"This is boring!"

"Mac, if you say one more thing I swear I am going to tell you things about your parents that you will never forget."

"Okay."

"So, do you kids understand so far? In the future you are American idiots and you own a bar. People get around by using these things called cars, which run on gasoline. Now guess what."

The boys sit staring at Nietzsche. Nietzsche looks back blankly. Then he rises up in his seat like a bear and scowls at them with his massive eyes and then his huge mustache twitches and Charlie recoils and says, "What!"

"Gasoline costs a lot of money. And in the future the prices start going up a lot because of international geopolitics and market fluctuations and who the hell knows what else. So you three, in the future, at your bar, come up with a plan."

The boys sit and stare at Nietzsche. "What's our plan?" Dennis asks.

"Do you really want to hear it? It's rather idiotic and self-deceiving."

"Yeah."

"No, you don't."

"Yeah I do, I promise."

Nietzsche chuckles. "What a joke. Okay, I'll tell you anyway. But not because you want me to."

How to Solve a Gas Crisis

"All-right, you imbeciles, let me tell you what you were destined to do in this story. He who has ears to hear, let him hear, hah hah. Are you awake? I'm ironically quoting Jesus."

The boys sit and stare.

"Okay, whatever. So one day Charlie is working at your stupid bar. Since Charlie isn't the brightest, he's decided that he's going to buy gasoline to run a generator engine to make electricity instead of getting electricity from an electric company, and use that engine's electricity to power the lights in the bar. They are all electric lights. This is the future."

Charlie frowns with an open mouth and says to himself, "I'm such an idiot."

"Mac and Dennis, you aren't so clever either but you intervene anyway to stop Charlie from using his gasoline-powered electricity generator since gasoline is expensive. More expensive than electricity, even."

Mac and Dennis high-five over Charlie's head. Charlie shudders at the loud clap over him.

"At this point things get worse. Mac, drunk on his own cleverness, makes up a plan to solve the problem of the gas price crisis—not even to 'solve' it, but to take advantage of it to your own benefit!"

Mac tries to high-five Dennis again but Dennis isn't paying attention, leaving Mac to impotently wave his hand over Charlie's head.

"Dennis, you are a seducer."

Dennis pumps his fist and it hits Mac's high-five hand by accident. They look at one another in confusion.

"But you're awful at it. No subtlety, charm, wit, or anything, really. It's awful. But it's still what you were fated to be. So you decide to create charts—charts!—with made-up statistics and images of women with enormous breasts, all to convince a bank manager to give you all a loan so that you can buy gasoline!"

Nietzsche coughs into his fist for several seconds.

"Mac's idiotic plan, by the way, is to buy gas in a large quantity, wait for several months, and sell it for a profit after prices go up."

Mac yells out "What a great plan!" and Charlie punches him in the shoulder.

"No, it is a ridiculous plan. You haven't actually gotten any brains."

Mac's smile remains on his face for a moment, like a ball at the top of its arc, and then falls into an open-mouthed frown.

"Now listen, you hobgoblins," Nietzsche chuckles. "Mac's idiotic plan fails. Of course it does. Not only do you three fail to seduce the bank manager—a woman, which you did not expect—but when you purchase gas anyway, you not only are unable to return it, but you fail to sell off any of what you purchase. Also, Charlie sets Mac's head on fire."

Charlie mouths "Yes" and nods. Mac cocks his head to one side and frowns.

"After these failures, Dennis decides to take over your group and declares himself to be the actual brains. To sell the gasoline you now own and recover some of the money you spent—money you stole from your sister, Dennis!—you decide to steal a van, which is a kind of ugly car, to sell gasoline at different individual houses. This is also a very stupid plan."

Dennis frowns. Charlie is raptly attentive, nodding, his mouth slightly open. Mac has been frowning since earlier, when he started frowning.

Nietzsche shakes his head. "At the first house you visit, Charlie tries to charm your interlocutor into purchasing gasoline, but he makes it sound as though you all mean to do terrible things to her. So you flee as she contacts the authorities to put you in prison." He is still shaking his head. "Seriously, you idiots never do a single thing right and it is amazing that you are alive at all."

For whatever reason, all three boys smile and nod their heads. It looks as though they are bobbing to a rhythm only the three of them can hear.

"I bet you're hoping for a good ending, eh? Well you're not going to get one. You idiots go into a water closet to piss and see your weird friend and co-owner of your bar, Frank, torturing Dee, Dennis's sister."

"Awesome," Dennis says.

"Shut up, Dennis. In this filthy room, redolent of feces and ammonia, you argue over your failed plan but become curious about Frank. You find that he and Dee were trying to work on another plan to frame a man for planning to do violence to untold numbers of people, and decide that you can incorporate this plan into your own plan while also incorporating Frank and Dee into your team."

Nietzsche winds up and kicks Mac in the arm after noticing that Mac had slumped forward and started to doze. Mac jerks awake.

"Wake up, you dolt. This part concerns you. At this point, Mac decides on the new plan: go along with Frank and Dee's plan to frame a person for terrorism, collect the reward money from turning him in to the authorities, and use the reward money to buy more gasoline. Because your foolish gasoline dream is still alive."

Charlie breathes in and screams, "I'm hungry!"

"Shut up and listen, Charlie. You are all inside the vehicle, with Mac driving, when something goes wrong. What do you think goes wrong?"

"We aren't driving fast enough!"

"We took the wrong route!"

"We summoned a vector imprecision matrix buffer slippers gazebo!"

"Wrong, Mac. Wrong, Dennis. Charlie, you were close, but still wrong."

"Damn," Mac says. He scrunches his eyebrows.

"What happens is, Charlie sabotages the vehicle so it cannot stop, and then he jumps out. Everyone jumps out. The van crashes and explodes, destroying much of your intended target's property for no reason. All of you walk away. That's the end."

Nietzsche leans back in his chair.

"He who has ears to hear, let him hear." He looks out the window at the bare branch again.

The boys stare. Finally, Dennis speaks.

"What in the actual hell does any of that mean?"

How to Solve a Crisis in Metaphysics

"None of you is very clever, are you?" Nietzsche asks. Mac and Dennis frown at him intently; Charlie looks out the window at the branch that Nietzsche has been looking at. "I want to put my nose in a silver sock," Charlie says. His eyes widen into a look of surprise. He had not meant to say anything out loud.

"Doesn't everyone," Nietzsche murmurs at the window.

Mac and Dennis are clenching and unclenching their firsts and screwing up their faces. Mac finally stands and says, "Uncle Fred, tell us what this story means or I'm going to throw you into the fire!" Dennis stands and raises his own voice, saying "You'll burn, just as you will in hell!"

"Oh stop it. What a couple of idiot children you are," says Nietzsche, not yet looking away from the window. "But I'll tell you anyway. Sit down and shut your stupid mouths."

The boys sit down and shut their stupid mouths. Charlie looks at the ceiling and starts to hum "Ride of the Valkyries."

"We'll go back to the beginning of my story," Nietzsche says, "and I will reintroduce you." Mac and Dennis are frowning; Charlie is looking at the ceiling and his mouth is open.

"We start with the problem. What is the problem? The gas situation is the problem. And why is it a problem? Because in this future world, the gasoline crisis opposes your idiotic purposes, which are to make money and live "high on the hog," as Americans sometimes say. Each of you wants pleasures such as these."

Dennis nods sagely, still frowning.

"The gasoline crisis in the story is like the world. And you three witless peacocks are like philosophers."

Dennis nods even more sagely.

"Why is this? It is because you try to come up with a scheme that makes sense of the world while benefiting you. A plan that is completely delusional."

Dennis nods, gripping his chin with one hand and crossing his free arm over his chest. He appears so sagely that one might be tempted to offer him a cup of hemlock, so as to ease his intellectual burden.

"Think about this, Mac. You name yourself the brains of your operation—an outrageous joke on a first look, until one realizes the context in which the assertion was made—and announce that you are going to "solve" the crisis. You mean to divine the "true" meaning of it, and reap a reward for doing so."

Frowning, Mac nods.

"You call yourself logical and denounce illogic while turning a blind eye toward the absurdities invoked by your own plan. Consider Dennis's poster, the one you prepared before meeting the bank manager to ask about a loan to purchase your gas."

Dennis nods, smiling. "I have to say, that was a great—"

"Shut up, Dennis," Nietzsche says, "and listen. The poster was ugly, ridiculous, and inane. But that's not the point. The point is how you used it. You try to cover over the utter stupidity of your proposal with distracting images of women with massive breasts. When the truth doesn't announce itself, only at that point is it necessary to convince your interlocutor of your case. And at this point we are already in dissembling and manipulation, regardless of our willingness to accept this."

Nietzsche eyes the boys in front of him.

"The reason for this is that our logic—our great powers of reason—developed lately in our evolution. Logic is a tool for survival, just like any of our other faculties. Truth and falsehood are irrelevant to it; survival value is the most important feature of logic. Mac's scheme doesn't capture the truth of the gasoline crisis in the story. But it doesn't need to. It need only provide a way for you three to acquire the things you desire. Reason and logic are just a gloss."

Nietzsche leans forward, eyeing the boys even more intently.

"And nowhere is this more apparent than in your breakdown at the bank. You absolute imbeciles! Rather than see the failures in your scheme, you degraded yourselves for a bewildered audience: you danced with your shirts off! Instead of seeing the failure of your scheme you danced with your shirts off at the bank!"

Dennis shifts in place. "But Uncle Fred," he says. "I had a new plan then, didn't I? To correct the mistakes?"

"Yes, you did. And it failed too. But each time you idiots failed, you also failed to recognize the true nature of the problem."

"And what's that?" asks Mac.

"That your schemes—your "paradigms"—are all doomed from the beginning. They are impositions of order on a world in which that order is foreign. Did you know anything at all about the gas crisis? No. There was nothing for you *to* know, but much to be gained from attempting to know it."

Nietzsche continues. "People used to believe that logic inhered in reality, that there were fundamental principles of organization structuring the world and leading up to God himself—and all their own moral values, by some happy chance. But within the last few centuries that whole edifice was blown away. Every theology and philosophy, like your paradigm, is an expression of will—an attempt to achieve some selfish end, no matter the pretentions to ultimate knowledge or appearances of moral praiseworthiness."

Charlie yawns, leaning back until he is about to fall.

"Charlie," Nietzsche says.

"Yeah?"

"Charlie, you are another reason why Mac and Dennis's plan fails."

"Hey, what are you talking about?"

"Listen and I'll tell you. Recall how obsessed you all became with the idea of "paradigms" during this failed escapade. Each of you had a designation: Mac christened himself the brains, Dennis the looks, and Charlie—you were named the wildcard. This is important. Even with how stupid they are, Mac and Dennis recognized that there was something about you they couldn't anticipate or contain, but they wanted you to have a role. What were you supposed to do? They were going to leave that up to you."

Nietzsche pauses and looks out the window again at the bare branch.

"They saw in you something wild and uncontainable, and still tried to harness that energy. Clearly, this is a self-defeating gesture. By incorporating you as the wildcard into their paradigm, they are planting the seed of destruction into their plan because you, the true wildcard, cannot be wrangled by any plan."

Charlie leans forward, mouth open, and stares at Nietzsche.

"Because you are idiots, I'm going to put this in clear terms. The ancient Greeks revered many gods, among them

Apollo and Dionysius. Apollo was stately and austere, evoking the clean lines of geometry and forms that recall the abstract philosophies of Pythagoras and others. Dionysius was, by contrast, wild and vital and not subject to containment. Her worshipers would cast aside notions of propriety and undertake such amazing, wanton orgies!"

Nietzsche holds his fist up and looks wistfully into the distance. Mac and Dennis nod their heads, smiling. Dennis looks at Mac and mouths, "Oh yeah. Sex orgies. I love doing those."

Nietzsche looks down at them. "Shut up, Dennis. You've never been with a woman in your life."

Dennis continues nodding and smiling, mouthing "Sex orgies, man. Sex orgies," and so forth. Nietzsche shakes his head and continues.

"Apollo and Dionysius, of course, represent two sides of ancient Greek culture. There's the orderly and abstract side, and the wildly indulgent and unrestrained side. You can see your gas scheme in the same way: Mac and Dennis make a two-headed Apollo, and Charlie—Charlie is Dionysius. The fatal problem with Apollonian schemes is the lofty idea that they might contain the wild energies of Dionysius, which they simply cannot."

Wide-eyed, Charlie sits and nods in assent. Mac frowns. Dennis is still nodding, smiling, and mouthing "sex orgies" at Mac.

"Charlie nearly brings ruin to the plan each time he acts. He threatens to blow up a gas station, makes intonations of perverse violence, and finally rips out the brakes from the van and jumps out the back. What a perfect symbol the van becomes! Everyone jumps out when they realize that it is doomed, as it has been from the beginning, and it crashes into an uninvolved person's car and explodes. Charlie and Mac, your system of thinking—your metaphysics, your grand scheme—literally blows up in your faces because you could not account for the wild and wanton force of Charlie."

"Yeah. Yeah!" Charlie says, nodding vigorously.

Charlie, the Proto-Superman

"Ah Charlie. You are the only worthwhile one in front of me."

"What? That's crazy," Mac says, "Charlie is an idiot."

Nietzsche sighs. "You do not understand," he says. "Charlie is a sign of things to come for the human race, provided you do not destroy yourselves completely in the coming century."

Wide-eyed once again, Charlie starts nodding at Nietzsche, and smiling, and then nodding and smiling, and then nodding and smiling and shouting "Yeah!" and pushing Dennis and Mac. "Yeah! A sign of things to come!"

Nietzsche leans forward and smiles darkly. "Charlie, yes, you are a sign. Your innocence, your malice, your creativity—your willingness to dominate others, to found your own values in the ongoing expression of your life and vitality. You are too innocent to know resentment. You still experience shame and embarrassment at the hands of others, but truly, you show me a sign of the coming of the Übermensch, who will make the rest of humanity seems like chattering apes beset with petty moralities and embittered with resentment."

"I sound awesome!"

"You? You are not, not yet. But if you were to become awesome, it would be by your own will, according to your own design, and in spite of whatever thoughts anyone has about you. You will have become yourself."

Nietzsche leans back into his chair and looks again out the window at the bare branch, tapping against the windowpane in the wind.

"Why am I so clever?" he says to himself. "I know why."

Charlie is smiling and bobbing in place. Mac and Dennis yawn deeply at the same time and get up to leave.

"Thanks for the story or whatever, but we've got to go," Dennis says. "There's this recycling thing we're doing. That's where you use trash over again instead of throwing it away? Anyway, it's going to make us a ton of money, so."

"Okay. You can leave."

Mac and Dennis leave.

"They will never learn," Nietzsche says to Charlie, "and will forever continue to scheme, and will be foiled again and again. But perhaps, even if their lives were to eternally recur in an identical fashion, they would still wish to live in the exact same way."

The rain continues outside unabated, the bare branch tapping at the window as Nietzsche looks on and Charlie furtively buries his face in a silver-stained sock, a can of spray paint lying on the floor behind him.

A Gallery of Real-Life Scumbags

ROBERT ARP

Each member of the gang shows varying degrees of dishonesty, egotism, selfishness, greed, pettiness, ignorance, laziness, and unethical behavior, and they are often engaged in controversial activities. Episodes usually find them hatching elaborate schemes, conspiring against one another and others for personal gain, vengeance, or simply for the entertainment of watching one another's downfall. They habitually inflict mental, emotional, and physical pain.

So reads one of the paragraphs in Wikipedia's entry on *It's Always Sunny in Philadelphia*, and whoever wrote this definitely nailed it. Below are examples of real-life dishonest, egotistical, selfish, greedy, petty, ignorant, lazy, and generally unethical people.

DISHONEST PEOPLE
Homo Dishonestens

In a well-written article from 2008 in the *Journal of Marketing Research* called "The Dishonesty of Honest People: A Theory of Self-Concept Maintenance," the authors give several examples of dishonesty, cheating, deception, and other forms of unethical behavior that are widespread today in business, government, sports, schools, and many other arenas.

In the US it's now commonplace for big corporations to be knowingly dishonest by breaking laws with the intention of asking for forgiveness and simply paying government fines for doing so later. While the media often focuses on extreme cases of cheating and sensational scams such as the Enron scandal or Madoff's Ponzi scheme, less attention is paid to what researchers call *ordinary* unethical behavior. Examples include stealing stuff from big stores like Walmart, not reporting income on one's taxes, buying clothing with the intention of wearing it once and returning it, taking all kinds of supplies from one's employer, or cheating on an exam. (Believe it or not, people in the US steal a sh@t ton of toilet paper and cheese—go figure.)

Through several tests that they set up, the authors of the article confirm what we already know: lots of people will give in to the temptation to be dishonest if they think they can get away with it, even those will "higher" moral standards, like religious folks.

In Plato's most famous work, *The Republic* (around 428–423 B.C.E.), one of the main issues discussed by Socrates and his Gang has to do with the idea that even good people will do dishonest and even horrible things, if they can get away with it.

In Book II, one of the participants in the discussion, Glaucon, tells the story of Gyges of Lydia, who was a mere shepherd in the service of the king of Lydia. Gyges finds a ring in a cave and discovers that the ring gives him the power to become invisible by turning it on his finger. He then proceeds to use his new power of invisibility to seduce the queen, and get her to help him murder the king so he himself can become king. The story is supposed to emphasize the fact that if someone has no fear of being punished, then they will do all manner of self-centered, self-serving, and wicked things.

Now, the question becomes this, which Socrates, Glaucon, and Adeimantus discuss in the rest of *The Republic*: It's easy to see how some scumbag shepherd could do dishonest and other evil things with lots of power, but what about someone who's already a totally moral, law-abiding, upstanding person? Can a basically good person be corrupted absolutely with absolute power? A lot of people—smart researchers, too—would say, "Hell, yes!" There have been numerous other articles and books in the past twenty-five years that present evidence showing what dishonest bastards we can be. Maybe this is part of the reason why the Gang's actions both repulse *and* delight us.

Fancy a Spot of (Stolen) Tea?

"British people are more likely to steal hotel towels and make false insurance claims than any other nationality," claimed a 2004 study from the *Journal of Consumer Marketing*. Blimey! These wankers apparently steal lots of stuff from restaurants, shops, and workplaces, and nearly half think it's okay to change the price tags on shopping items as well. Plenty of those polled also would drink a can of soda in a supermarket and not buy it, report a lost item as stolen to an insurance company to collect the money, use an employer's telephone to make private calls, not say anything when charged too little in a restaurant, rent a double-bed hotel room and use it for more than two people, and steal toiletries from the cleaning trolley in a hotel, too.

The researchers also found that, compared with other religions, Christians were most likely to favor unethical behavior! Jesus Christ! And it didn't matter if people were male or female. The researchers were from UMIST (University of Manchester Institute of Science and Technology), and quizzed consumers in London, other parts of Europe, the US, and the Far East. "We make great statements about our moral superiority—especially compared with wicked, rapacious Americans," note the British researchers. "Yet, when it comes to basic ethics—making a clear distinction between right and wrong—we fall well behind standards in the USA."

Definitely *not* a good show, chaps . . .

. . . Pants on Fire

Pathological liar, compulsive liar, habitual liar, chronic liar, and mythomaniac are all names for someone who fibs about literally every aspect of their life. They lie about bigger things like having met a celebrity, run a marathon, or obtained a degree from an Ivy League school, and they lie about minor things like what they ate last night, when the last time the dog was bathed, or who they talked to recently.

Pathological liars generally suffer from low self-esteem and definitely aren't rooted in reality. They lie so much that it's become a way of life to make up things for a variety of reasons—eventually the truth actually becomes uncomfortable while the made-up, lied-about, fantasy world of their own mind feels right to them. It's sad, really. And it's incredibly frustrating for the people around the pathological liar who have to deal with the BS. Eventually, these mythomaniacs are ostracized and rejected, primarily because they can't be trusted.

Rob Arp (the co-editor of this volume, in case you forgot) dated someone who most likely was a pathological liar when he was in high school in the mid-1980s, as she would make up sh@t like crazy. Eventually she cheated on Rob and he had to kick her to the curb. It was devastating to him at the time, no doubt! Recently, he noticed on Facebook that almost thirty years later she's still a BS-er making outrageous claims about what she's been up to over the years.

Here are some (in)famous liars, perhaps some of them mythomaniacs:

RICHARD NIXON (1913–1994) was the thirty-seventh President of the US, and his name is virtually synonymous with Watergate . . . and dishonesty. Not only was this Commander in Chief involved in illegal activities in the early 1970s—including wiretapping, harassment of political opponents, and knowledge of attempted burglaries and wiretapping of the Democratic National Committee headquarters in the Watergate Hotel complex in

Washington, DC—but he also lied and tried to cover up the misdeeds. The truth eventually came to light; or to sound, really, since there were taped recordings of Nixon talking about his lies and cover-ups. He resigned on August 9th, 1974 before he could be impeached. "I am not a crook," he famously claimed (and people have lampooned ever since). Yeah, right . . .

JAMES FREY wrote a supposed autobiography called *A Million Little Pieces* (2003) about his life as a twenty-three-year-old alcoholic and drug abuser coping with rehabilitation in a treatment center. It became a bestseller thanks to Oprah Winfrey, who selected it for her book club. However, it came out that important parts of the book had been fabricated. After much controversy, Frey appeared on the *Oprah Winfrey Show* for the second time on January 26th, 2006 and claimed that the "demons" that had driven him to abuse alcohol and drugs were the same ones that had led him to invent events in his autobiography. Oprah told him: "I feel that you betrayed millions of readers."

STEPHEN GLASS wrote for the *New Republic*—a liberal American magazine of commentary on politics and the arts published continuously since 1914—in the 1990s. A movie about Glass called *Shattered Glass* came out in 2003 starring Hayden Christensen as Glass. The tagline for the movie was: "He'd do anything to get a great story." Why? Because he had made up at least half of the stories he reported!

Glass had gone so far as to create fake websites and sources as well. He also got others to play along with and corroborate his lies. The editor of the *New Republic* at the time, Charles Lane, had this to say after Glass was fired:

We extended normal human trust to someone who basically lacked a conscience. . . . We busy, friendly folks, were no match for such a willful deceiver. . . . We thought Glass was interested in our personal lives, or our struggles with work, and we thought it was because he cared. Actually, it was all about sizing us up and searching for vulnerabilities. What we saw as concern was actually contempt.

The Glass scandal is not the only one for the magazine, however: *New Republic* editor from 1948 to 1956, MICHAEL WHITNEY STRAIGHT, was later discovered to be a spy for the KGB; in 1995 *New Republic* writer RUTH SHALIT was fired for repeated incidents of plagiarism and an excess of factual errors in her articles; *New Republic* senior editor LEE SIEGEL maintained a blog on the *New Republic* site dedicated primarily to art and culture in 2006, and it turns out he was posting comments to his own blog under an alias praising himself while attacking his critics, even claiming not to be Lee Siegel when challenged by an anonymous blogger; and there are other *New Republic* scandals. . . .

JANET LESLIE COOKE used to work for *The Washington Post* until it was discovered that a Pulitzer Prize-winning story that she had written titled "Jimmy's World"—about an eight-year-old heroin addict—was a fable she had concocted. In order to get the job at the *Washington Post*, Cooke also falsely claimed to have a degree from Vassar College and to have studied at the Sorbonne in Paris. In 1980 the assistant managing editor of the *Washington Post* at the time, Bob Woodward, submitted "Jimmy's World" for the Pulitzer Prize for Feature Writing, and Cooke received the award on April 13th, 1981. (Incidentally, Woodward and Carl Bernstein were young reporters at the *Post* in the early 1970s, and it was their investigating and reporting that helped crack open the Nixon Watergate scandal.)

"It is a brilliant story—fake and fraud that it is . . ." claimed Woodward in a press release shortly after Cooke resigned and returned the Pulitzer. In 1996 Cooke sold the movie rights in the story to Tri-Star Pictures for $1.6 million, but the project apparently never moved past the script stage.

BILL CLINTON was the forty-second President of the US, and his name is almost immediately associated with Monica Lewinsky, of whom Clinton claimed, "I did not have sexual relations with that woman." He lied. In 1998 Clinton became the second president in US history (the first was Andrew Johnson) to be impeached by the US House of Representatives. He was charged with perjury and obstruction of justice, but was acquitted of both charges by the US Senate on February 12th, 1999. Clinton later admitted he had "misled people, including even my wife. I deeply regret that." Yet he never officially apologized for his actions.

For years Lewinsky has claimed that Clinton and she engaged in a "consensual relationship" despite her being painted by Clinton and his allies as a stalker during the scandal. Lewinsky maintained the proverbial "It takes two to tango" in a May 2014 issue of *Vanity Fair*. Clinton may make nice-nice with Lewinsky more than fifteen years after the scandal so as to insulate former First Lady Hillary Clinton from bad press in Mrs. Clinton's 2016 presidential bid.

HIERONYMUS CARL FRIEDRICH BARON VON MÜNCH-HAUSEN (1720–1797) was a German nobleman and one of the most famous bullsh@tters of all time. Or, he was an innocent person who told tall tales purely for entertainment, and was then misrepresented by the real villain, Rudolf Erich Raspe, as being the king of all bullsh@tters. One or the other.

Baron Münchhausen reportedly told people that he rode a horse underwater, escaped from a swampy morass by pulling himself out by his own hair, rode cannonballs across the sky, and traveled to the Moon.

Two psychological disorders are named after him: *Münchhausen syndrome* is a disorder in which someone feigns illness in order to get attention. *Münchhausen syndrome by proxy* is a disorder in which a caregiver (usually the mother) fakes or induces illness in her child or in another person in her care in order to gain attention and sympathy. Google "The Münchhausen Mom" and you'll be directed to a 2008 case where the lead investigator claimed:

I've been in law enforcement for thirty years, and I have never encountered anything like this before.

Why did he say this? Because he had met LESLIE WIL-FRED, a woman who made up her pregnancy with twins and made up their stillborn death too. A search of her computer revealed that Leslie had ordered Huggable Teddy Bear urns five days prior to the twins' "deaths," indicating she had planned to concoct the stillbirth story all along. And there are tons more cases like this one, even worse in terms of the lies and the effects of the lies on family and friends.

Now Google MARYBETH TINNING and you'll see someone claim that this was the "worst Münchhausen syndrome by proxy case in history." That's because she likely killed all nine of her children: two-week-old Jennifer in 1972; two-year-old Joseph, Jr. seventeen days later; four-year-old Barbara six weeks after that; three-week-old Timothy in 1973; six-month-old Nathan in 1975; four-month-old Mary Frances in 1979; four-month-old Jonathan in 1980; two-year-old Michael in 1981, and four-month-old Tami Lynne in 1985.

She eventually confessed to smothering Tami Lynne, Nathan, and Timothy (which she later retracted), and the other kids all supposedly died of SIDS and other "natural causes." What's even more amazing than the fact that a mom would do this to her own children, however, is the fact that in all that time—from 1972 to 1985—no medical people or anyone else thought to call the cops and push for a serious investigation of this serial killer until she had ended the life of her ninth child.

EGOTISTICAL PEOPLE
Possibly the Biggest Egomaniacs Who Ever Lived

Let's do an old fashioned matching game here. Try to match the egomaniacal quotation to the egomaniac:

EGOMANIAC	EGOMANIAC'S EGOMANIACAL QUOTATION
Kanye West	*"My job is not to be easy on people. My job is to make them better."*
Glenn Beck	*"It's hard being the NBA's sex symbol, but somebody has to do it."*
Dennis Reynolds	*"As a man who works very hard to maintain a certain level of physical excellence, . . . I find shortcuts insulting. Now give me a piece of ham now!"*
Paris Hilton	*"Part of me suspects that I'm a loser; the other part thinks I'm God Almighty."*
Charlie Kelly	*"I don't wanna hear about your dreams, okay? I hate listening to people's dreams. It's like flipping through a stack of old photographs. If I'm not in any of 'em and nobody's having sex, I just, I don't care."*
Shaquille O'Neal	*"I was in the Vatican and they knew who I was, 'Of course we know who you are,' they said. 'What you're doing is wildly important.'"*
Frank Reynolds	*"It's really stupid. But people are stupid too, so . . ."*
Steve Jobs	*"My greatest pain in life is that I'll never see myself perform live."*
Alec Baldwin as Blake	*"I think every decade has an iconic blonde—like Marilyn Monroe or Princess Diana—and right now, I'm that icon."*

(continued)

Robert Arp, PhD (in philosophy)	*"I have a different constitution. I have a different brain; I have a different heart; I got tiger blood, man."*
Charlie Sheen	*"I done told you once, you son of a bitch, I'm the best that's ever been."*
Mac McDonald	*"So, am I the Messiah? I don't know. I could be. I'm not ruling it out."*
Johnny from GA	*"Well, someone has to bag my groceries. I'm not gonna do it. I have a friggin' PhD in philosophy, god dammit!"*
Dee Reynolds	*"See, I would have gone in and bought a box of magnum condoms, thus demonstrating I have a monster dong."*
John Lennon	*"Fuck you. That's my name. You know why, mister? You drove a Hyundai to get here. I drove an eighty-thousand-dollar BMW. THAT'S my name."*
Yngwie Malmsteen	*"I am (the Messiah, the Son of the Blessed One) . . . and you will see the Son of Man sitting at the right hand of the Mighty One and coming on the clouds of Heaven."*
Jesus Christ	*"I'm so good, Eddie Van Halen is afraid to meet me."*

Moms and Mother Theresa

We're all naturally concerned with our own welfare, security, and happiness. Self-preservation is basic for any animal, and humans are no different. There are countless examples of actual events—many now caught on tape and shown on reality TV shows—where a person is getting mugged, or knifed to death, or is run over by a car, and the F-ing jerkoffs witnessing the event (or the aftermath) do nothing but watch as the horrible events unfold. When asked afterward why they didn't help the victim, the typical response of the jerkoff is: "Hey, I'm not gonna risk my life" or "It's not my problem."

When we survey the entire *It's Always Sunny* show thus far, we can see a gazillion examples of Frank, or Charlie, or

Mac, or Dennis, or Sweet Dee—or any number of other characters on the show—acting like self-centered dicks who wouldn't lift a finger to help someone else unless there was something "in it for" them. "Charlie Has Cancer" from the first season comes to mind as a perfect example of basically everyone acting selfishly to lesser and (mostly) greater degrees.

However, *should* everything we do or not do *always and at all times* be done with an eye toward our own personal benefit or pay-off? If you answer yes to this question, then you're likely an ethical egoist. The ethical egoist puts forward an argument that goes something like this:

Premise #1: Look around you: it's a dog-eat-dog, rat-race-like, cruel kind of world. Each and every person is always out for her/his own good, and, further, you'll get screwed over by people if you don't look out for your own good.

Premise #2: If it's true that every person is always out for her/his own good, then each and every one of us *should* be out for our own personal good.

Conclusion: Therefore, each and every one of us *should* always be out for our own personal good. In other words, we should all be ethical egoists.

However, this argument for ethical egoism has been rejected for a number of reasons. First off, Premise #1 is debatable. Is it really true that each and every person is *always* out for their own good? *Always*? What about moms and Mother Theresa? How about firemen and first responders? Aren't they examples of people who are concerned for others?

Now, the ethical egoist could respond here by saying something like this: "You have to look deeper into the real psychological motivations for people's actions. When you do, you see that self-preservation and selfishness are what *really* motivates, and it just *seems* that people are acting self*less*ly. Moms take care of their kids or even will die for their kids because if they didn't they would feel horrible, get put in jail, and/or be shamed by others for not doing so. So, it's not really about their kids, it's still really about *them* and the sense of pride and accomplishment *they* have in raising *their own* kids properly, or the sense of failure *they* have in poorly raising their kids. Moms, just like all people, are really—at root—self-centered. And firemen get paid to run into buildings and die, so again it's about *themselves*, the money *they* make, the job *they're* doing, and what will happen to *them* if *they* don't do *their* jobs. And Mother Theresa? *She* helped the poor and worked with victims of AIDS so that *she* could get into heaven, and not go to hell and burn for eternity, which is *the* most self-centered of reasons to act! It was all about *her own* eternal salvation!"

This response stems from the idea that there's no way *whatsoever* that a person could be anything other than self-centered and self-concerned. In one sense, it's not possible to test whether this is true because it's hard to get at what *exactly* really motivates people to act in certain situations, as any professional psychologist will tell you.

You could respond back to the ethical egoist with more examples of people who seem to act selflessly—people who ran into the World Trade Center and died on 9/11, the guy who was killed by the rapist while coming to the aid of a woman being raped, the woman who herself fell in the raging river and dies, trying to save a stranger—and the ethical egoist will always respond with: "It *looks* as if someone is being selfless, but deep down it's basic self-preservation or self-interest that motivates anyone to act one way or another."

There are some acts that sure seem pretty selfless. It's hard to imagine that the mom who pushed her child out of the way of a speeding car, only to save her child and get run over dead herself in the process, was acting purely out of a selfish reason! She friggin' died and knew she ran that risk! If the ethical egoist is right, then we'd want to preserve our lives at all costs, and even a mom would be like, "I'm not dying for my kid," allowing the kid to be run over. In fact, any act of bravery where someone dies as a result of helping or saving someone else seems to fall into this selfless category. It's the selfish person who *would do absolutely nothing*. Look at the *inactions* of Frank, or Charlie, or Mac, or Dennis, or Sweet Dee, when they should be acting—now *that's* selfishness! Maybe the ethical egoist is *partly* correct in that there's an admixture of egoism in every action committed; otherwise we wouldn't act in the first place? But it's hard to imagine that acting for the self is the *sole* reason for acting *at any and all times.*

Premise #2 of the ethical egoist's argument is: If it's true that every person is always out for their own good, then each and every one of us *should* be out for our own personal good. There are many problems with this claim that make it suspect, but we'll just mention one here. First, just because something *is* the case, does not mean that it *ought to be* the case, which I am sure we have all heard on more than one occasion. For example:

- Just because it *is* the case that the class doesn't want to take the final exam does not mean that they *shouldn't* take the final exam. The final likely is integral to the class and the grading system utilized, for example.

- Just because it *is* the case that you want a fifth piece of cake doesn't mean that you *should* have the fifth piece of cake, for obvious fat-ass and other health reasons.

- Just because it *is* the case that someone "turns you on" doesn't mean that you *should* sleep with them, especially if you're married!

- Just because it is the case that Charlie and Mac can steal Frank's money from his secret bank account doesn't mean they *should*.

So too, even if it were the case that everybody was a self-centered devil, this doesn't mean that they *should* act devilish toward one another. In fact, to a certain extent there are "little devils" running around already: they're called children. Kids are naturally self-centered, but that doesn't mean that they should be. When Sally kicks Johnny in the package for no good reason at school, Ms. Smith the teacher doesn't say, "Kick him again, Sally, then punch him in the kidney while he's rolling on the ground in pain, so he pisses himself!" No. She disciplines Sally so she learns that she shouldn't do something like that.

Our lives would be complete misery and there would be total chaos if each one of us always acted with only the self in mind. The devil-kid problem is highlighted in the famous story by William Golding, *Lord of the Flies*, where some kids are stranded on a deserted island for a period of time. Eventually, the kids run around wreaking havoc, burning things, and killing each other because they are little egoists with no sense of the "other's good," and no societal laws enforcing laws for the benefit of all the people who comprise their situation. No one wants that kind of environment in which to live, so ethical egoism would be just plain horrible if truly enacted. The selfishness exhibited by the Gang on *It's Always Sunny* fascinates us and, in a bizarre way, is so repulsive that we want to keep watching in morbid anticipation to see the next totally selfish thing that one of them will do.

SELFISH PEOPLE
Selfish Pricks

The two defining characteristics of selfishness are being concerned excessively or exclusively with oneself and having no regard for the needs or feelings of others. Selfishness and egoism are similar to one another, in fact, and it could be argued that they mean the exact same thing. But since the person who wrote the Wikipedia entry listed selfishness as one of the qualities that the Gang exhibits, we're gonna hit it as well. Look at the way basically everyone acts in the Season Two episode "Dennis and Dee Go on Welfare," for example, with Dennis and Dee selfishly taking advantage of the welfare system in the US, and Charlie and Mac selfishly stealing Frank's secret stash of money and spending it on hookers at an extravagant party.

One of the biggest selfish pricks to ever walk the Earth was a guy named CHARLES PONZI (1882–1949), of Ponzi scheme fame. Remember "The Great Recession," from Season Five of *It's Always Sunny*? Frank claims he lost all of his money in a Ponzi scheme, which is an investment scam where the scammer gets people to invest money by giving it to the scammer (someone like Chucky P) to invest, but the scammer never invests it and instead pays dividends back to the investors from *new* investors' money. The scammer lies and says he's invested the money, but he hasn't. In other words, the scammer pays returns to investors from new capital paid to the scammer by new investors, rather than from profit earned by the investors' investments. Of course, the scammer takes a cut of the money up front for having "invested" it. Selfish pricks who operate Ponzi schemes usually entice new investors by offering higher returns than other investments, in the form of short-term returns that are either abnormally high or unusually consistent. The perpetuation of the high returns requires an ever-increasing flow of money from new investors to sustain the scheme, obviously.

Chucky P's scheme had to do with promising clients a fifty-percent profit within forty-five days, or one-hundred-percent profit within ninety days, by buying discounted postal reply coupons (PRCs) in other countries and redeeming them at face value in the US to make a profit. The purpose of the PRC was to allow someone in one country to send it to a correspondent in another country, who could use it to pay the postage of a reply. International PRCs were priced at the cost of postage in the country of purchase, but could be exchanged for stamps to cover the cost of postage in the US; if these values were different, there was a potential profit. In reality, Ponzi was paying earlier investors using the money of later investors, and never purchased most of the PRCs. In 1920, at times he was making $250,000 a day, which equates to a cool $3 million today!

Now, there are at least three ways a Ponzi scheme goes south. First, the schemer can simply high-tail it out of the country or into hiding with all of the money, effectively screwing over all of the investors by straightforwardly stealing from them. Ponzi schemers normally don't do this because they know they can continue to fleece folks and make more and more money. The second way a Ponzi scheme goes south has to do with the inflow of investments from new folks slowing down to the point where the schemer can't pay dividends back to the older generation of investing folks, and those folks say, "Hey, where's the money you promised?!?" and the jig is usually up. That may have happened to Frank. He may have been one of the poor suckers who invested with a schemer later in the game, and when other earlier folks started asking the schemer for their money and the schemer paid them with Frank and other latecomers' money, the scam was revealed, and there wasn't any money left to pay Frank (since the scammer gave it all to older investors) *or* the US Government seized the scammer's money—either way, Frank would have been left with zilch. The third way a Ponzi scheme goes south usually occurs during a sharp decline in the economy, which causes many investors to withdraw part or all of their funds from the schemer, and the money quickly runs out, and, again, the jig is up. This also may have happened to Frank.

Do you recall former stockbroker, investment advisor, and financier Bernie Madoff? He was the chairman of the NASDAQ stock market for a while, as well as the admitted operator of a Ponzi scheme that is considered to be the largest financial fraud in US history with estimated actual losses to investors of $18 billion! The third way a Ponzi scheme goes south is precisely what happened to Madoff during the market downturn and Great Recession of 2008. Folks were losing money, freaked out, and then wanted their investments back from Madoff, and he simply couldn't deliver. The *It's Always Sunny* episode "The Great Recession" plays off of this immense scandal, obviously. On June 29th, 2009 Madoff was sentenced to 150 years in prison, the maximum allowed for such a prick-like crime. Some people who lost money as a result of Madoff's Ponzi scheme committed suicide, others died of heart attacks, most had to alter their lavish lifestyles, all are still fighting legal battles today, to recover at least some of their investments, one died of a stroke, and at least one elderly person lost so much that she has had to eat cat food in order to survive.

The Public Be Damned!

WILLIAM HENRY VANDERBILT (1821–1884) is a name most of us have heard because he was one of the richest men who ever lived, being an American businessman and philanthropist who owned several US railroads in the nineteenth century. About two years before he died, he was on his private railroad car just about to eat dinner when a young freelance reporter, Clarence Dresser, entered the car and demanded an immediate interview. "Don't you run your railroad for the benefit of the public?" Dresser asked. To which Vanderbilt famously replied, at least according to Dresser:

> The public be damned. What does the public care for the railroads except to get as much out of them for as small a consideration as possible. I don't take any stock in this silly nonsense about working for anybody's good but our own, because we are not. When we make a move, we do it because it is our interest to do so, not because we expect to do somebody else some good. Of course we like to do everything possible for the benefit of humanity in general, but when we do we first see that we are benefiting ourselves. Railroads are not run on sentiment, but on business principles and to pay, and I don't mean to be egotistic when I say that the roads which I have had anything to do with have generally paid pretty well.

Vanderbilt probably was an ethical egoist.

Robert Arp

Selfish Selfies

A selfie is a self-portrait usually taken with a hand-held phone or digital camera that almost always winds up on Facebook, Instagram, or some other social media-sharing site. At times a person will take the photo with something memorable or famous in the background, but often the shot is taken simply for the "Look at me! I look fantabulous!" or "Look at me! I'm so important!" or "Look at me! I'm so deep!" factor. Teenagers are the most notorious selfie takers, and there's a famous selfie you can find on the Internet that the Grand Duchess Anastasia Nikolaevna of Russia took in the mirror not long before she was executed along with her entire tsar family in 1918 by the commie reds in the Russian Revolution.

BAHSID MCLEAN made headlines in 2013 when a selfie surfaced of him smiling and holding his dead mother's head, which he had sawed off after stabbing her to death because she told him to grow up and go get his own apartment. McLean created a Twitter handle called @kill-tanyabyrd and a MySpace page called "Kill the bitch Tanya" in order to display the selfie and announce to the world what he had done. Mclean and his friend, William Harris, used a power saw to chop up Tanya Byrd's body; her head, torso, hands, and legs were found by police in plastic bags strewn among garbage in South Bronx. Tanya Byrd's sister, Cassandra McLean, told the *New York Daily News* that a few weeks before the crime, Byrd caught her son scouring the Internet for "how to" tips on covering up a murder. In court, Bahsid McLean had to wear a plastic bag, then Depends, because he kept pissing on himself, and he told the judge that he didn't do anything wrong: "My mom was dying anyway, so I just helped her along."

"Woman Snaps the Most Selfish Selfie Ever" is the title of a 2013 story in *The New York Post* of a woman who took a selfie with a man in the background on the Brooklyn Bridge; the man was threatening to jump into the freezing-cold water below during the holiday season. The woman had stopped along with around a hundred other spectators and reporters to watch as police tried to talk the suicidal man off of the suspension wires that support the bridge over the East River. The man eventually was talked off the bridge. "What's your name?" asked one of the *Post* reporters who witnessed the sunglass-bedecked, Park-Place-looking blonde take the shot. "I'd rather not say," the blonde claimed as she quickly skedaddled out of there, apparently realizing that what she had done might be viewed as self-absorbed and insensitive.

SPIDEYNIKKA is Florida high-school student Malik Whiter's Twitter handle, and in October of 2013 he tweeted a selfie of himself sporting an immense grin as his pregnant teacher can be seen at her desk in the background on her cellphone call to 911 as she writhes in pain holding her head. "Selfie with my teacher while she's having contractions," accompanied the tweeted picture, and it became a viral sensation. A Google search of "SpideyNikka" yields parody images of Mr. Nikka's grinning face with Jesus carrying the cross in the background, the situation room of President Obama and his cabinet watching the Osama bin Laden raid with Hillary Clinton looking shockingly sad, or the Hindenburg disaster. Even though what SpideyNikka did seemed selfish, the memes are actually funny as hell.

PRESIDENT BARACK OBAMA shocked numerous folks during Nelson Mandela's funeral when he was caught on camera taking smiling selfies with Danish Prime Minister Helle Thorning-Schmidt and British Prime Minister David Cameron. People thought it was in "poor taste" since it was taken during the funeral event. However, in Obama's defense, South Africans made a big deal about how the event should be more like a celebration, and it wasn't like Obama took the photos while folks were eulogizing Mandela up at the podium. Maybe Obama should have taken a selfie with that friggin' crazy guy who was pretending to sign what Mr. President was saying. Gotta love that thorough South African security!

GREEDY PEOPLE

Acquisitiveness, avarice, covetousness, cupidity, and *rapacity*—these are all words synonymous with *greed*, which can be defined as the desire to possess objects, goods, or wealth to an extravagant extent—well beyond basic needs or even wants—and to keep these possessions for oneself. The old miser who's visited by the Ghosts of Christmas Past, Present, and Future, Ebenezer Scrooge, from *A Christmas Carol* comes to mind as a clear example of a greedy person, and so does Gordon Gekko (played by Michael Douglas) from the movie *Wall Street* with his famous "Greed is Good" speech. Below are actually greedy folks from the annals of history.

MARCUS LICINIUS CRASSUS (115–53 B.C.E.) was born into a wealthy Roman family around the year 115 B.C.E. and acquired enormous wealth through "fire and rapine," in the words of Plutarch. By the time he died, Crassus supposedly increased his sizable inheritance of seven million sesterces (a sesterce is a Roman coin worth about $3.50 in modern monetary terms) to a fortune of about 170 million sesterces (about $600 million), or a sum nearly equal to the entire annual income of the Roman treasury! It's been claimed that he was the wealthiest person in Roman history. This guy was one greedy prick, apparently. He rented land, purchased slaves, had them trained, and then sold them for handsome profits. He also took advantage of the fact that Rome had no fire department. Ancient Rome was overcrowded and, frequently, fires would destroy entire neighborhoods. Crassus created his own fire brigade of five hundred men who would rush to burning buildings at the first cry of alarm. Upon arriving at the scene, the fire fighters did nothing while Crassus bargained over the price of their services with the distressed property owner. If Crassus couldn't negotiate a satisfactory price, his men simply let the structure burn to the ground.

However, the bulk of Crassus's enormous wealth consisted of his vast landholdings, acquired while he was a lieutenant to Lucius Cornelius Sulla during the civil war of 88–82 B.C.E. Sulla became dictator of Rome and allowed Crassus to buy captured enemy property at bargain prices, but the acquisitive Roman wasn't satisfied with this alone and proceeded to seize the estates of magnates *not* on the proscribed list, often killing the innocent owners. When his greed surpassed every civilized limit, Crassus lost Sulla's support. Nevertheless, through loans to nearly every Roman senator and lavish entertainments for the populace, Crassus succeeded in acquiring what he wanted most—political power.

During the last years of the Roman republic, he formed the First Triumvirate with Gaius Julius Caesar and Gnaeus Pompeius Magnus. Greed proved fatal to him, as Crassus got killed during a disastrous military campaign—the Battle of Carrhae in 53 B.C.E.—when he wanted to conquer the Kingdom of Parthia, famous for its wealth. His legend for being a greedy bastard preceding him, the Parthians cut the head off of Crassus's corpse and filled the mouth with molten gold to finally "satiate Crassus's unyielding thirst for wealth."

GHENGHIS KHAN (1162–1227) rose from humble beginnings to establish the largest land empire in history— four times larger than the empire of Alexander the Great. He was born with the name Temujin, and only later chose the name Genghis Khan, meaning "Universal Ruler." After uniting the nomadic tribes of the Mongolian plateau, he conquered huge chunks of central Asia and China. At their peak around 1225, the Mongols under Khan's rule controlled between eleven and twelve million contiguous square miles, an area about the size of Africa, and the Mongolian Empire stretched from the Sea of Japan to the Adriatic.

Many people were slaughtered in the course of Khan's invasions, but he also granted religious freedom to his subjects, forbade the selling and kidnapping of women, abolished torture, made livestock theft punishable by death, abolished inherited aristocratic titles, encouraged trade, ordered the adoption of a writing system, conducted a regular census, granted diplomatic immunity to foreign ambassadors, and created the first international postal system, all of which helped to organize, unite, and strengthen his empire. The Mongols would show up at smaller towns, villages, and cities en masse and offer the folk the opportunity to surrender or die a horrible death, and this terror-inducing strategy usually worked. When it didn't, the Mongols slaughtered most of the people, allowing a few to go spread the word to the next town . . . where the Mongol terror strategy would *definitely* work! They would then slaughter the leaders and soldiers of the town, spare everyone else, give them jobs, put a few Mongols in charge of the town, then ride on to the next conquest.

In 1246, Ghengis Khan's grandson, Guyuk Khan, received an envoy from Pope Innocent IV. In a letter carried by the envoy, the Pope told Guyuk about Jesus, the Church, the various Commandments, and how he, the Pope, was the official voice of God. The Pope also told Guyuk that he should stop broadening the Mongol Empire since the Catholic Church was the rightful ruler of all the Earth. Finally, he offered the entire Mongol community the opportunity to convert to Catholicism. Guyuk proceeded to slaughter most of the Pope's envoy, and sent who was left back to the Pope with the message that God had given the Mongols, not the Pope, control of the Earth, "from the rising sun to the setting sun." God, Guyuk claimed, intended the Mongols to spread His commandments in the form of Genghis Khan's Great Laws, the ones that worked so well under his grandfather's rule. "You must submit to me," Guyuk told the Pope, "and you will . . . when I arrive there soon." Guyuk died in 1247, however, and the Mongols began fracturing into smaller divided kingdoms. Within one hundred years, the Mongols lost control of almost all of the areas they had conquered.

FRANCESCO DELLA ROVERE (1414–1484) accomplished quite a lot during his tenure as Pope Sixtus IV: he commissioned the Sistine Chapel; he helped usher the Early Renaissance into Rome by having the Vatican Archives constructed; he annulled the decrees of the Council of Constance; he also ordered the inconceivable torturing of infidels with iron maidens, anal pears, and other horrible devices through the Spanish Inquisition; he was part of a plot to kill members of the de' Medici family (and succeeded in killing one); he sanctioned slavery through the authority of the Church; he had at least two male lovers; he was an ephebophile too, having had sex with numerous male mid-to-late adolescents, generally ages fifteen to nineteen; he was a pimp and brothel-owner; oh, and let's not forget that the greedy bastard lined the pockets of the Catholic Church with something called *indulgences*. Essentially, an indulgence would give you time off in purgatory, which is where Catholics believed you went to cleanse your soul after you died and before getting into Heaven. Almost everyone was going to have to "serve some time" in the Big P, so you'd want to serve as little time as is possible before getting your eternal bliss with God Himself. Indulgences could be earned through charity work, or going on a Crusade—or they could be bought. The Catholic Church took advantage of the buying power of indulgences and, in fact, this is one of the main reasons why Martin Luther (1483–1546) was so pissed off and the Protestant Reformation began on October 31st, 1517 when Luther posted his Ninety-five Theses on the door of the Castle Church of Wittenberg, Germany.

Three more greedy pricks from history include William M. Tweed (1823–1878), the Empress Dowager Cixi (1835–1908), and Imelda Marcos (1929):

"Twas Tweed who stole all of the peoples' money" was how one nineteenth-century political cartoon cleverly depicted WILLIAM M. TWEED (1823–1878), a bank, railway, hotel, and landowner in New York who was also known as "the Boss" of one of the most egregious and flagrant examples of political corruption in American history, the Tammany Hall Democratic Party. In fact, during 1870–1871 Tweed was featured in close to one hundred cartoons in *Harper's Weekly* showing him to be a greedy and corrupt bastard, by the guy known as the Father of the Modern Political Cartoon, Thomas Nast. "Stop them damned pictures!" Tweed is reported to have said. "I don't care so much what the papers say about me. My constituents don't know how to read, but they can't help seeing them damned pictures!" Tweed tried to bribe Nast with $500,000 (that would be $9.6 million today!), but Nast refused. Tweed became known for wearing a large diamond in his shirtfront and lived in a mansion on Fifth Avenue, and it's estimated that he defrauded the Big Apple out of between $30 million and $200 million—that's $365 million to $2.4 billion today! It's probably the case that Nast's constant political pictorial portrayal (you like that alliteration?) of the corruption of the Boss and his Tammany Hall cronies in his cartoons set in motion events for Tweed which included investigation of his corruption, his arrest, his re-election, his trial, his re-trial, his jail time, his escape from jail, his capture in Spain, his second round of jail time, and his death in NYC's Ludlow Street Jail on April 12, 1878 from severe pneumonia.

The EMPRESS DOWAGER CIXI started her career as a whore of the Chinese Emperor Xianfeng in her adolescence, eventually giving birth to his son. Once Xianfeng died in 1861, Cixi's son became emperor and essentially

Cixi ran China behind the scenes. She is said to have had diamonds and other gems placed on the floor of her bedroom in between her bed and where her shoes were kept so that her feet would always touch the finest of things; her shoes were made of a lavish material and had sewn diamonds and other jewels on it. She had three thousand jewelry boxes, and she used the Chinese navy's money to build herself a marble banquet boat where she could eat lavish dinners with chopsticks made out of pure gold. Unsatisfied with her own tomb, in 1895 she ordered its destruction and reconstruction. The new tomb was a lavish grandiose complex of temples, gates, and pavilions, covered with gold leaf, and with gold and gilded-bronze ornaments hanging from the beams and the eaves. Eventually, twenty years after Cixi died, in 1928 robbers came into the tomb and took the jade objects, coral, silver, gold, diamonds, and other precious stones placed in and around her sarcophagus. They ravaged the corpse itself, taking her imperial robe, underwear, shoes, and socks, and all the pearls and jewels on her body. They even pried open the corpses' mouth and took the large pearl that had been placed there for Cixi's trip to the afterlife. You really *can't* take it with you, can you?

"I was born ostentatious. They will list my name in the dictionary someday. They will use *Imeldific* to mean ostentatious extravagance." This is a quotation from the Associated Press of the Tagalog wife of President Ferdinand Marcos, **IMELDA MARCOS**. Not only has she been suspected of having stolen—along with her husband—over $5 million from the Philippine people she ruled from 1965 to 1986, but also, when she and her husband were deposed from power in 1986, authorities found over a thousand pairs of shoes in museum-like cases inside huge rooms dedicated to them in Malacañang, the presidential palace. Her actual total shoe ownership has been estimated at three thousand. Imelda's extravagance was beyond any acceptable limit, no doubt. *Newsweek* magazine put her on their 2009 list of Greediest People of All Time. During an expedition to purchase real estate in New York City in the early 1980s, she considered, then rejected, buying the Empire State Building (estimated to cost around $750 million at the time) because it was too glaring and "ostentatious"—instead, she bought the $51 million Crown Building, the $60 million Herald Centre, and other pieces of prime real estate in Manhattan. All were subsequently seized and sold by 1987, as were much of her jewels and the bulk of the art she had collected over the years. But she got to keep the shoes. . . .

Petty People

Pettiness can be defined as being narrow-minded, or showing too much attention to frivolous things, or it can even refer to meanness of spirit generally.

Stella! Stelllllllllllllaaaaaaaa!!!

In the August 17th, 1994 ruling *Liebeck v. McDonald's Restaurants*, a New Mexico civil jury awarded $2.86 million Stella Liebeck, a seventy-nine-year-old woman who suffered third-degree burns in her netherlands when she accidentally spilled hot coffee in her lap after purchasing it from a McDonald's restaurant. In 1992 she and her grandson ordered the forty-nine-cent cup of java through a Mickey D's drive-thru window, and they parked the car so Stella could put cream in her coffee. She placed the cup between her thighs and spilled it on herself after trying to take the top off. She had third-degree burns, poor thing, and had to be hospitalized with skin grafts and whatnot for an extended period of time. Back then, there wasn't the "This is hotter than sh@t" notification written all over Mickey D's' coffee cups and lids. The first thought on almost everyone's mind after they heard about the multi-million-dollar verdict in Stella's favor was: Are you F-ing kidding me? It's crazy and unfair that Mickey D's should have to pay out money in a lawsuit for something that a person did of her own free will. Was McDonald's really responsible for how Stella handled her coffee? Stella's attorney argued that McDonald's was "grossly negligent" in selling "unreasonably dangerous" and "defectively manufactured" coffee. It worked, mostly—the court ruled that Mickey D's was eighty percent responsible for Stella's burns. After a few appeals, both parties settled out of court for an undisclosed amount that is known to be no more than $600,000. Since then, people have tried, but failed, to sue Mickey D's and places like Starbucks, Chick-Fil-A, Dunkin' Donuts, Wendy's, Burger King, numerous hospitals, and other establishments over hot coffee that *they* spilled on *themselves*! Most of these lawsuits occurred in the US, of course, since we Yanks are such a litigious society. Some have argued that this case—as petty as it appears to be—actually was an important step in tort law in the US, which requires those found to be at fault for harming others to compensate the victims, usually in money. Plus, it caused basically every kind of hot cup and attending lid sold from an establishment to have CAUTION: CONTENTS ARE EXTREMELY HOT written on it . . . in case you forgot that you ordered something extremely hot in the two minutes since you ordered it.

Motion to Kiss My Ass

If you watch just a few episodes of any legal drama on TV in the US, you'll likely hear a lawyer in a trial say something to the judge like, "Your Honor, I move to dismiss these charges" or "Your Honor, I want you to know that I filed a motion to dismiss." In the US legal system, a motion is a formal way of bringing an issue before the court for consideration, usually by a lawyer on behalf of their client. There are all types of standard motions in the US legal system. In the mid-1990s a Georgia inmate named Matthew Washington filed some seventy-five motions, one of which was simply "Motion to Kiss My Ass" which he filed out of anger given that all the seventy-four other motions weren't ruled in his favor. There's generally no cost to file a motion, but in

Washington's case the courts finally said he had to pay $1,500 the next time he wanted the courts to "move" on (or consider) any of his claims. That was the end of his motions. . . .

Ignorant People

Ignorance can mean 1. lack of knowledge, but it can also mean 2. lack of knowledge when *someone should know better*, as when someone is foolish, moronic, or stupid. The following is a list of ignorant people in the "lack of knowledge" *and* in the "stupid" sense; however, as you'll see, some are probably mo' stupider than others :>)

550 B.C.E.: Legend has it that the Brazen Bull was designed and constructed by a Greek brass worker named Perilaus of Athens in the sixth century B.C.E. and offered as a gift to Phalaris (around 570–554 B.C.E.), the tyrant ruler of the province of Agrigento on the southern coast of present-day Sicily. It was a hollow bronze statue crafted to resemble a real bull with a door on the side large enough for a person to enter. It also had a series of specially designed pipes placed inside the head as well as vents in the bull's nostrils. A victim was placed inside— usually after having his tongue cut out—and the door was shut and locked from the outside. Fires would then be lit around the bull. As the victim was being roasted alive within, smoke from burning flesh, hair, and clothing would exit the bull's nostrils, and he would thrash about and scream in agony; thus, the sights and sounds of this spectacle simulated an angry, snorting, growling, bellowing bull that was about to charge. Perilaus claimed the bull had the twofold (paradoxically sadomasochistic) purpose of deterring crime and entertaining those who witnessed the device put to use.

In a bizarre twist of fate, Perilaus was actually the first person to experience the horror of his own invention. According to the story as it is told by the rhetorician and satirist, Lucian of Samosata (around 120–180 C.E.), after

Perilaus presented the bull to Phalaris and noted that the victim's screams "will come to you through the pipes as the most tender, most pathetic, and most melodious of bellowing," Phalaris became disgusted by Perilaus's wicked cleverness and tricked him into entering the bull:

> His words revolted me. I loathed the thought of such ingenious cruelty, and resolved to punish the artificer in kind. "If this is anything more than an empty boast, Perilaus," I said to him, "if your art can really produce this effect, get inside yourself, and pretend to roar; and we will see whether the pipes will make such music as you describe." He consented; and when he was inside I closed the aperture, and ordered a fire to be kindled. "Receive," I cried, "the due reward of your wondrous art: let the music-master be the first to play!"

Phalaris removed Perilaus from the bull after he was satisfied that it worked fairly well and before Perilaus died, and had the brass worker thrown off a cliff to his death, so the story goes. Historians observe that it is strange that Phalaris would be revolted by Perilaus's invention since Phalaris was known to be such as cruel man and a "devourer of suckling infants." Then again, what Phalaris did to Perilaus was obviously cruel. By some reports, Phalaris himself became an eventual victim of the bull when his subjects grew tired of his mistreatment.

The Brazen Bull became one of the most common methods of execution in Ancient Greece and was co-opted by the Romans. During the prosecutions of Christians by the Emperor Domitian (81–96 C.E.), Antipas of Pergamum was roasted alive in a version of this device, becoming the first Christian martyr from Asia Minor in 96 C.E. With his wife and children, Saint Eustace was martyred in a brazen bull by the Emperor Hadrian in 118 C.E., and in 287 Pelagia of Tarsus was burned to death in one by Emperor Diocletian (245–311). Even the original dragon slayer himself, St. George (around 275–303), is shown in a four-part painting from around 1510 being roasted in a

brazen bull before being dragged through the streets behind a horse and beheaded. The bull was used very little
during the Middle Ages but would appear in accounts
during the Spanish Inquisition (1478–1834). More recently, the Brazen Bull concept has been adapted to horror films; one such device appeared near the end of *Saw
3D: The Final Chapter* (2010), and one in the shape of an
elephant is used by Father Solomon in 2011's *Red Riding
Hood*.

1008: Ismail ibn Hammad al-Jawhari was an Islamic
scholar who wrote an Arabic dictionary. He died when he
leapt from the roof of a mosque attempting to fly using a
flying device he built with his own hands: two wooden
wings and a rope.

1550: It's common knowledge that the Chinese invented
gunpowder and the first rocket-like missiles. And, of
course, fireworks. A Chinese government official name
Wan Hu attempted to launch himself into outer space in
a chair to which forty-seven rockets were attached. Think
of a typical fireworks display, and you can imagine what
happened next. . . .

1567: The Burgermeister (Meisterburger!) of Braunau,
Austria, Hans Steininger, died when he broke his neck
tripping over his own four-and-a-half-foot-long beard! He
must've been a short guy.

1863: Horace Lawson Hunley was a Confederate marine
engineer and inventor of the first combat submarine, the
CSS *Hunley*. He died during a third try at utilizing the
vessel.

1871: While defending his client during a trial, Ohio
lawyer Clement Vallandigham accidentally shot himself
in the courtroom while demonstrating how the victim
may have shot himself. The guy Vallandigham was

defending, Thomas McGehan, was ultimately cleared—Vallandigham, however, died from the self-inflicted wound.

1896: Otto Lilienthal died the day after crashing one of the hang gliders he designed and built.

1896: Sylvester H. Roper killed himself during a test run of his newly invented steam-powered bicycle.

1903: William Nelson was a General Electric employee who designed a new way to motorize bicycles and also died during a test run of his newly invented bike.

1912: Franz Reichelt jumped to his death from the Eiffel Tower while testing his invention, the coat parachute. It was his first ever attempt with the parachute, and he had told the authorities in advance that he would test it first with a dummy. He was the dummy all right! You can see the actual video on YouTube of the event captured on camera by the French press. Using a ruler, one guy measures how many inches deep the indention in the grass was after the body was carted away, and shows the camera.

1912: Thomas Andrews, Jr. went down on the RMS *Titanic*. He was the naval architect in charge of the plans for the *Titanic* and supposedly remarked to a colleague that the ship was "as nearly perfect as human brains can make her" just hours before it hit that darned iceberg.

1928: Alexander Bogdanov was a Marxist physician and science fiction writer who thought that blood transfusions were the key to immortality. After a few tries, colleagues commented that he looked ten years younger. Bogdanov didn't realize that his blood wasn't compatible with the blood of one of his students, unfortunately, and he died as a result of the transfusion.

1932: Fred Duesenberg was a German-born American automobile designer who killed himself in one of his own Duesenberg autos during an awfully fast test drive.

1944: Thomas Midgley, Jr. was famous for having developed tetraethyl lead as an additive to gasoline and chlorofluorocarbon. The poor guy contracted polio at age fifty-one which crippled him, but then devised a device of ropes and pulleys to help others lift him from bed. Four years later he would be strangled by this device after accidentally becoming entangled in it.

1973: The AVE Mizar was a flying car designed by a guy named Henry Smolinski made out of a Ford Pinto. It actually flew a few times. During a test flight with Smolinski at the "wheel," it crashed and killed the designer.

1984: Jim Fixx was the author of the 1977 best-selling book, *The Complete Book of Running*. He's credited with popularizing the sport of running and demonstrating the health benefits of regular jogging. He died of a heart attack on July 20th after one of his daily runs.

1985: Karel Soucek was a Canadian professional stuntman who developed a shock-absorbent barrel. In fact, he survived going over Niagara Falls in the barrel, believe it or not! He didn't survive a drop from the roof of the Houston Astrodome, however.

1985: The Darwin Awards come into being, where awards are "given posthumously to people who have made the supreme sacrifice to keep their genes out of our pool. Style counts, not everyone who dies from their own stupidity can win."

2009: The AVCEN Jetpod (just what it sounds like) was designed by British engineer, Michael Dacre, who died during a test flight of the flying vehicle in Malaysia.

2013: Five idiots were injured—one seriously—when their Tennessee trailer blew up due to the fact that one of the geniuses tried to flush their makeshift meth lab down the toilet while deputies knocked on the front door. Meth and moisture don't mix, and they shoulda known betta! If you Google "meth labs blow up" you'll be amazed at the number of kinds of things that have been blown up by meth labs, to include basements of houses, attics of houses, roofs of houses, wings of houses, rooms of houses, entire houses, basements of apartments, roofs of apartments, entire apartments, rooms of condominiums, roofs of condominiums, entire condominiums, rooms of townhouses, roofs of townhouses, entire townhouses, rooms of duplexes, roofs of duplexes, entire duplexes, garages, back rooms of business establishments, basements of business establishments, entire business establishments, backs of trailers, entire trailers, hotel rooms, motel rooms, hostels, cars, vans, busses, motorcycles, bicycles, tricycles, RVs, tractors, doghouses, cathouses (in the prostitute sense), and chicken coops. We sh@t you not. . . .

LAZY PEOPLE

Laziness is the unwillingness to work or utilize energy. The US is one of the laziest nations in the world when you consider how friggin' obese folks are. An obese person has an abnormal accumulation of body fat, usually twenty percent or more over their ideal body weight. A March 2014 *U.S. News and World Report* article puts the US at Number One in a top-ten list of most obese countries. Around a third of all US adults are chunky monkeys and more than a quarter of US kids are fatties, too. Why? Everyone knows why, and it's a very simple explanation. Because we're lazy—we eat high-calorie fast food meals instead of taking the time to cook; we don't regulate how much we eat; and we don't get enough exercise to burn off excess calories because we're sitting on our asses at work, at play, and most other times, too. Of course, some people have a genetic problem, or are severely depressed, or have some other problem beyond their control that makes them fat; however, most everyone who oinks got into the mess by themselves. Below are a few cases of lazy folks.

MANUEL "MEME" URIBE GARZA's liver and heart stopped working, and he died in May of 2014. He was in the Guinness Book of World Records for being the heaviest man alive at 1,316 pounds. That's almost as heavy as a stripped-down Ford Pinto from the early 1970s! He admitted that he ate crap all of the time and never exercised. Plus, he was depressed and his genetic disposition also had a part to play in his morbid obesity. Whereas a normal person would eat one or two bowls of Frosted Flakes and two cups of milk for breakfast, Meme would eat two boxes of Frosted Flakes and two gallons of milk for breakfast! Now that Meme is dead, Khalid bin Mohsen Shaarie of Saudi Arabia is the heaviest living person; he's currently at 1,340 pounds.

A man weighing over 500 pounds died after being found fused to his chair in his Bellaire, Ohio, home, where he had sat naked in a recliner for two years. Apparently, he couldn't get up, his girlfriend would feed him daily, and he would use a bedpan and pails to urinate and defecate in. His girlfriend found him unconscious one day in the spring of 2011 and called 911. The police and firefighters said that when they came to his home his skin was stuck to the chair's fabric, and he was infested with maggots and his own urine and feces. When they pulled the chair from his back, sections of his skin were ripped off and "had become one with the chair," as one of the paramedics noted. One cop described the scene as the "worst he ever responded to" and noted that he had to throw his uniform away after helping pry the man from the chair. Another copper threw up in the living room corner from the smell of the place. The conditions in the house were described as "deplorable" and "filthy," with cockroaches living in the walls, and field mice scattering in the kitchen. Emergency crews had to use a chainsaw to cut a hole in the side of his house and then hoist the guy onto a flatbed truck. Soon after arriving at the hospital, he died. Cockroach eggs were found in the folds of his fat.

Two twenty-one-year-old "parents" of a baby boy named Riley are currently serving sixty-year sentences in Texas jails for almost starving their one-year-old child to death. In December of 2012 several teens were attending a party at the couple's mobile home in rural Hood County, Texas, when they heard crying from the back of the trailer. What they found was baby Riley covered in urine and vomit, looking like a small skeleton covered with skin. They took Riley to the hospital, and he eventually made a full recovery after being fed intravenously for some time. Riley's parents admitted that they didn't want the responsibility of raising a kid and would rather smoke pot and party. They hadn't fed him sufficiently since he was born. Riley was adopted by a loving family, and within months he looked like a normal baby boy.

Thirty-five-year-old Pam Babcock in Wichita, Kansas wasn't lazy, really, but she apparently spent two years in her boyfriend Kory McFarren's bathroom on the pot, from the fall of 2007 to the fall of 2009, and literally became one with the toilet seat. "She was not glued. She was not tied. She was just physically stuck by her body. It is hard to imagine . . . I still have a hard time imagining it myself," Ness County Sheriff Bryan Whipple said in a telephone interview, adding that it appeared her body fat had grown attached to the seat. McFarren would bring Babcock food and water during the two years she was on the crapper and told investigators that he asked her daily to come out of the bathroom. She would reply, "Maybe tomorrow." Police found the clothed Babcock sitting on the toilet, her sweat pants down to her mid-thigh as if she was using the toilet. Her legs had atrophied. Paramedics pried the seat away from the toilet and, with the seat attached to the her rear, transported Babcock to the hospital where doctors surgically removed it. McFarren later claimed, "Pam and I had a normal relationship like anyone else . . . except that it was in the bathroom."

Unethical People

The English word *ethical* is derived from the Greek word (thikos) meaning "character" or "moral nature." The English word *moral* derives from the Latin *moralis* meaning "manner" or "custom." Nowadays, we use the terms *ethical* and *moral* interchangeably to refer to actions that are praised or blamed based upon whether they conform or don't conform to the rules of conduct recognized by a particular society, culture, or group.

Murdering, lying, stealing, raping, deceiving, and cheating are examples of unethical or immoral behaviors that basically every society, culture, or group on the planet finds worthy of punishment. Some actions are *so* highly unethical that we call them *despicable*, which means the same thing as abhorrent, abominable, awful, contemptible, detestable, hateful, heinous, loathsome, or reprehensible—in other words, dirty, rotten, lowdown, and scoundrel-like. Below are a few examples of real-life scoundrels.

It doesn't get much lower than this. When you lose a loved one, you post an obituary in the paper or on line, along with details of the wake, or funeral, or service you'll be attending. A scumbag reads the obit, waits until you're gone from your house, and then robs you. Sad to say, it happens all of the time, in every part of the world. It happened to Cindy and Dennis Higdon in the spring of 2013, who live in a small Kentucky town. Their poor son Christian was tragically killed, and three guys stole jewelry, computers, and even some of Christian's items from his room while Cindy and Dennis were at the cemetery burying the boy. They eventually caught the bastards. "It's heinous. It's reprehensible," said lead investigator Margaret Ludwig. (On a personal note, Rob Arp's brother, John, was killed in an auto accident in 1994, and one of his "friends" stole John's social security number to open up credit cards and get loans. That's f@cking low, too. The prick was caught and spent time in jail. A guy like that needs to have his kneecaps busted with a baseball bat in a back alley somewhere. . . .)

"Portland Woman Loses Savings in Upgraded Nigerian Scam" was a headline of a story in the spring of 2012 on the website of the NBC news affiliate in Portland, Oregon. A seventy-one-year-old woman got an email from someone in Nigeria claiming to be an American soldier who had procured a chest of gold and other valuable items that he needed to transport from Nigeria to Portland. He would share the wealth with the old lady once he arrived in three days. The email even came with a picture and phone number of a certain Dr. King. The woman withdrew $42,000 from her bank and wired it to Dr. King. When three days came and went, she got another email from Dr. King saying that he needed another $80,000 to transport the chest. He even called her to chat. When the old lady protested, he threatened her by saying that the chest was actually stolen and she was now complicit in a crime. She had better pay up, or he would go to the police. So she did. And there went her entire life's savings. When the old lady's daughter and others questioned the Wells Fargo bank where she kept her savings account, "Didn't you think it was strange that Grandma was withdrawing her entire savings account?" the bank manager said that he had asked her if she was completely sure that she wanted to go ahead with the withdrawal. "We can advise the customer," the manager said, "and we did for sure in this case. We can warn the customer, but in the end, it's their money and we can't refuse the customer their funds." It's obvious to most anyone nowadays that scoundrels are trying to scam folks through email, and that such scamming of innocents is abominable. Dr. King is yet another person who needs to have his kneecaps busted in a back alley. However, some have wondered whether the old lady's greed and willingness to engage in something that was fishy from the start (after all, the whole deal seemed illegal and unethical) made for an "It serves you right" situation for her.

TOM MABE was working in his Louisville, Kentucky, office when he began his personal crusade against telemarketers, fabricating elaborate stories to exasperate the phone solicitors to the point where they hung up on him. In time he began recording the calls on his answering machine and playing the tapes for friends; soon Mabe started appearing on radio morning shows as well, ultimately financing a CD collection of his best pranks titled *Revenge on the Telemarketers*, which came out in 2000. Rob Arp has listened to that CD several times. In one of the recordings, a guy selling funeral caskets calls Mabe, and Mabe pretends like he wants to kill himself. Now, Mabe pretending to be suicidal is pretty low, but what's even lower is the fact that the casket salesman asks Mabe if he could wait to kill himself *until he first purchases a casket*! They barter back and forth for several minutes with Mabe eventually agreeing to buy a moderately priced casket since, given that he plans to put a bullet through his head, "no one will see the inside of the casket because it'll be a closed-casket wake and funeral."

Bitches, It's the Authors in the Book, Bitches

KYLE ALKEMA, distant-future PhD, is as erratic as the Gang in places—one day interested in biotechnology, the next in super-heroes; one day in toxicology, the next in sitcoms. He eventually hopes to write a paper about everything he likes, but that would be a comedy in itself . . . bitches.

ROB ARP, PhD, is a philosopher-turned-government-contractor-turned-hopefully-philosopher-again-at-some-point. He's studied the physical. He's studied the metaphysical. He's even studied the pataphysical . . . bitches.

TIM AYLSWORTH is a philosophy PhD candidate at the University of Wisconsin-Madison. He mostly works on Kant, but he also likes to think about how not to be a sociopathic jabroni like Dennis . . . bitches.

ADAM BARKMAN, PhD, is Associate Professor of Philosophy and Chair of the Department of Philosophy at Redeemer University College (Canada). He's the author or co-editor of eight books, most recently *Making Sense of Islamic Art and Architecture* (2015) and *Imitating the Saints: Christian Philosophy and Superhero Mythology* (2014). While Barkman and his Gang of six family members do understand a thing or two about escalating situations, typically this leads to spontaneous days at the beach rather than breaking into houses and the like . . . bitches.

ETHAN CHAMBERS is a PhD student at Cardiff University. Theories of the self and virtue ethics feature heavily in his dram bach . . . bitches.

CHARLENE ELSBY, PhD, is an assistant professor at Indiana University-Purdue University Fort Wayne, teaching Popular Culture and Philosophy among other courses. That counts towards half a major . . . bitches.

RUSS HAMER is a graduate student at Marquette University focusing on Kierkegaard. When he gambles with his friends, they use an invented currency that has a variable exchange rate depending on how each one of them feels at the time. By doing this they create a self-sustaining economy. It's economics 101 . . . bitches.

ROGER HUNT just met someone with the last name Lefevre, and impulsively started taking troll foot photos . . . he sort of teaches philosophy, hopefully inspires young people to do philosophy, and a bunch of other Charlie work . . . bitches.

JASON IULIANO is a graduate of Harvard Law School. Like Charlie, he acts as if he knows a lot about the law and various other lawyerings. Currently, Jason is pursuing a PhD in Politics at Princeton. However, his real dream is to one day go toe-to-toe with Charlie on bird law . . . bitches.

MARTY JONES received his BA from Wheaton College and his MA from the Katholieke Universiteit Leuven. He is a master of karate, and friendship, for everyone . . . bitches.

CHRISTOPHER KETCHAM, PhD, is a reformed academic who lives contingently near Philly. He writes on social justice, philosophy and popular culture, and risk management where he has contributed to and edited two books. His current project is raising funds for the 666 Foundation of the Seven Churches that will hopefully gain beatification for Charlie. All donations are welcome. No burnt offerings, please . . . bitches.

SKYLER KING is an undergrad philosopher who is crossing the Bridge to Terabithia (or is it the scary bridge in Jersey Shore?) to grad philosopher. So, basically, he is one or two big steps away from being called up to the major leagues. But don't worry. He hasn't tried to sneak into the majors through an underground tunnel like the Gang tried to do for the Phillies game. Instead, he has just done some super dope things like publish witty and nutty philosophy papers in various volumes of the *Popular Culture and Philosophy* series and in undergraduate journals. His primary interests are ethics (in general), global systems, and linguistics/philosophy of language. That's what's called a trifecta, jabroni. A trifecta . . . bitches.

CHARLOTTE KNOWLES is a PhD student in Philosophy at Birkbeck College, University of London, where she works on Heidegger and Feminist Philosophy. When she's not busy philosophizing, Charlotte spends her time experimenting with new meat and alcohol combinations, perfecting her super badass roundhouse kicks, and attempting to patent "Chardick Mikeard"—her very own version of the game of games—an enterprise in which her extensive knowledge of bird law has proved invaluable . . . bitches.

DANIEL "DAYMAN" LEONARD is a teacher and writer from Flipadelphia, Pennsylvania. He has master's degrees in philosophy, poetry, karate, and friendship. He enjoys the occasional milk steak.

GREG LITTMANN, PhD good. Is associate professor of philosophy at SIUE. Publish metaphysics, epistemology, philosophy of logic!!! Also. Write many chapters philosophy popular culture, including on *Adventure Time, Big Bang Theory, Boardwalk Empire, Breaking Bad, The Daily Show,* and *Doctor Who.* All spelled good. Good Littmann. You money him now and womans . . . bitches.

FENNER TANSWELL is a philosophy graduate student in St Andrews and Stirling, thinking about math and logic, which often make him their bitch. In his spare time he plays the game of games and fights crime . . . bitches.

Index

absolute power corrupts absolutely, 180–81
Achilles, 6–11, 14–15
ad hominem fallacy, 153–54
Agamemnon, 6, 9, 12, 16
"The Aluminum Monster vs. Fatty McGoo", 10, 18, 72–73, 96, 129
"America's Next Top Paddy's Billboard Model Contest," 6, 9
angels, 33
"The ANTI-Social Network," 11
Apollo, 176
appeal to inappropriate authority fallacy, 154–55
argument, 147–157
Aristippus, 22, 23, 25, 27
Aristotle, 4, 22, 32, 33, 34, 37, 80, 92, 93, 99, 155, 160
Artemis, 70
asshole (or ass), 3–5, 7–9, 11–13, 15–17, 19, 123, 127, 131
atheism, 32, 33
attitude pairs, 38, 39
authenticity, 67, 68–69, 71, 73, 74

beatification, 31, 32, 33, 34, 35, 37, 40, 41
bitches, 15, 57, 75, 155–56, 159–160, 162, 165–66, 188, 196, 217–19
"Bums: Making a Mess All Over the City," 18, 97, 140
burden of proof, 152–53

canonization, 31
Catholicism, 87–88
CharDee MacDennis, 3, 9, 13, 55–58, 63, 64, 161
"CharDee MacDennis: The Game of Games," 3, 9, 13, 55–58, 64, 161
Charlie, 3, 5–7, 9–16, 18, 23–30, 31–41, 46, 48–50, 57–59, 63, 79, 81–89, 91–101, 105–06, 115–19, 123–130, 133–141, 150–54, 160–62, 165–178, 187–89, 191–93, 218
"Charlie and Dee Find Love," 12, 94
"Charlie Gets Crippled," 12, 69, 82, 84, 88, 99, 135
"Charlie Goes America All Over Everybody's Ass," 16, 17, 46, 95

"Charlie Got Molested," 9, 23, 46, 50, 85, 87

"Charlie Has Cancer," 11, 84–85, 135, 189

"Charlie Kelly: King of the Rats," 13, 67, 123

"Charlie's Mom Has Cancer," 11, 15

"Charlie Rules the World," 3, 7, 9, 10

"Charlie Wants an Abortion," 15, 17, 74, 87

cheating, 12–13, 16, 56, 179–182

choice, 32–40, 46, 67–69, 71, 73, 80–81, 93, 96, 120–21 128, 130, 173

Colin, 38

conscience, 86

consent, 114, 116, 117, 120

contingency, 32, 34, 35, 37, 38, 39, 40

cosmological explanation, 32

Country Mac, 74

courage, 22, 80

creepiness, 45–53

cultural script, 69–70, 72, 73

Dee, 3–15, 18, 21–22, 24, 26, 30, 35, 36, 40, 45, 55–58, 61, 63–74, 79–89, 91, 93–97, 99, 101, 106, 108, 115–120, 123, 127–29, 133–141, 143, 148, 152, 156, 160, 167–178, 183, 185, 188–193

"Dee Gives Birth," 141

"Dee Reynolds: Shaping America's Youth," 16

Dennis, 3–4, 6–15, 21–27, 35, 40, 48, 70–73, 72–75, 113–17, 119–122, 159–166, 167–178

"The D.E.N.N.I.S System," 3–4, 12, 60, 84, 98, 103, 105, 107, 109, 148, 159

"Dennis and Dee Go on Welfare," 3, 12, 25, 26, 68, 74, 82–83, 135, 144, 188, 192

"Dennis and Dee's Mom is Dead," 133

"Dennis Looks Like a Registered Sex Offender," 68, 73

"Dennis Reynolds: An Erotic Life," 8, 9, 95

Descartes, René, 104, 156

Dionysius, 176

donkey brains, 150–52

empiricism, 103–04

equivocation fallacy, 156

ethics; *see* morals

evolution, 153–56, 159–160, 162, 165–66, 174

Experience Machine, 28–29

fallacies, 149, 152–55

falsification, 160–62

family, 15–18, 22, 51, 95, 119, 127, 135, 149, 154, 186, 196

Fatty McGoo, 10, 18, 129

"Feast of Fools," 39

feminism, 138–140

"Flowers for Charlie," 14, 28, 81

Frank, 3, 5–6, 8–9, 11–15, 18, 21–27, 35–40, 56–59, 62, 68–69, 73–75, 82–86, 91–101, 104, 127–130, 135, 137, 139, 142, 144, 147, 150–51, 159–160, 171, 187–88, 191–94

"Frank's Back in Business," 22

"Frank's Pretty Woman," 10, 21, 96–97, 100

free will, 32–40, 46, 67–69, 71, 73, 80–81, 93, 96, 120–21 128, 130, 173

friendship, 3, 5–6, 8, 10–11, 13–14, 17–18, 38, 58, 65, 70,

79, 87, 95, 97, 110, 124, 127, 137, 149, 171, 183, 186, 196, 212–18

games, 3, 6–7, 9–10, 12–13, 16, 41, 55–63, 65, 136, 143, 161, 187, 194
"The Gang Broke Dee," 13–14, 95
"The Gang Buys a Boat," 25, 26, 73, 98, 113–14, 147, 157
"The Gang Dances Their Asses Off," 12–13
"The Gang Desperately Tries to Win an Award," 5, 10
"The Gang Exploits a Miracle," 12, 24, 26, 31, 164
"The Gang Finds a Dumpster Baby," 83, 88, 143
"The Gang Gets Extreme: Makeover Home Edition," 135, 142
"The Gang Gets Held Hostage," 14, 46–50, 119–120
"The Gang Gets Racist," 5, 8
"The Gang Gets Stranded in the Woods," 72
"The Gang Gets Successful," 73
"The Gang Gets Whacked," 12
"The Gang Gives Back," 16
"The Gang Gives Frank an Intervention," 68, 69
"The Gang Goes to Jersey Shore," 69, 119
"The Gang Makes Lethal Weapon 6," 5
"The Gang Recycles Their Trash," 26
"The Gang Runs for Office," 12, 27, 87, 144
"The Gang Saves the Day," 5, 7
"The Gang Solves the Gas Crisis," 4, 26, 162, 169–178

"The Gang Squashes Their Beefs," 25
"The Gang Wrestles for the Troops," 16, 25
generosity, 22
glory, 5, 8–11, 17–18
God, 3–7, 13, 16, 31, 32, 34, 35, 37, 47, 87–88, 104–05, 119, 125–27, 160, 175–76, 187–88, 200–01
Golden Mean, 80
goodness, 1–54, 83–89, 95–96, 123, 125–26, 136, 138–143, 153–56, 159, 161, 163, 165, 180–81
"The Great Recession," 5, 14, 139
Greek mythology, 3–19
grotesque, 39
"Gun Fever," 3, 7, 37, 81, 87
"Gun Fever Too: Still Hot," 3, 7–8, 16, 39–40
"Gunther's Guns," 39

happiness, 5, 14, 18, 23, 29, 58, 79–80, 88–89, 94–99, 138, 175
hedonism, 22–30
hedonistic paradox, 29–30
Heidegger, Martin, 65, 74, 75
"The High School Reunion, Part 2: The Gang's Revenge," 11, 72–73
Homer, 4, 13–14
Homeric values, 4–19
honesty, 22
"How Mac Got Fat," 73, 87–88, 96
Hume, David, 103, 123–24, 126, 128, 131
"Hundred Dollar Baby," 97

Iliad, 4, 8–10
immutability, 34, 35

implication, 113–14, 120–22
impossibility, 37
inauthenticity, 65, 68, 70, 72, 74
incest, 50–51
individualism, 67
inquisition, 33
irrationality, 26

jabronis, 23, 116, 122, 133, 135,
    137, 139, 141, 143, 217, 219

Kuhn, Thomas, 163–65

Lil' Kev, 117–18
logic, 22, 39, 46–50, 58–62,
    107–08, 125–131, 147–157,
    165, 173–75, 182, 185, 189
lying, 19, 38, 55, 61, 65, 69–70,
    104–06, 129–130, 178

Mac, 3–4, 6–11, 14–15, 17–18,
    21–27, 35, 40, 55–59, 63–69,
    73–74, 79–89, 91–93, 96–101,
    113–122, 125–130, 133–143,
    147–48, 151–57, 159–166,
    167–178, 188–89, 191–92
"Mac and Charlie Die (Part 1),"
    14, 130
"Mac and Charlie Die (Part 2),"
    14, 130
"Mac and Dennis Buy a Time
    Share," 4
"Mac Day," 6, 8, 73–74, 96
"Mac and Dennis Break Up," 30,
    74
"Mac and Dennis: Man Hunters,"
    7, 24–25, 28, 69, 101, 134
"Mac Day," 6, 8, 73–74
"Mac Fights Gay Marriage," 74
"Mac Is a Serial Killer," 73

"Mac's Banging the Waitress,"
    11, 74
"Mac's Big Break," 68
Mathis, Bruce, 136, 138, 139, 143
"The Maureen Ponderosa
    Wedding Massacre," 48, 51
the McPoyles, 45–53, 119–120
metaphysics, 123, 172–77
milk, 51–52
Mill, John Stuart, 29
mind, 56–59, 67, 72, 108–09, 119,
    124–25
money, 4–5, 17–18
moral concept, 75
moral relativism, 51
morals, 4, 17–19, 21–23, 25, 51,
    60, 75, 81, 87–89, 91–93, 99,
    101, 111, 114–18, 122–131,
    133–144, 147, 164, 175, 177,
    180–81
mythology, 3–19

necessity, 32, 34, 37, 38
Nietzsche, Friedrich, 167–178
Noddings, Nel, 138–140
normal science, 163
Nozick, Robert, 28–29

obstinate, 162
Odysseus, 4–10, 12–13, 15–17
Odyssey, 4–5, 15
orgy, 176

Paddy's, 4–6, 9, 12, 16, 22, 41,
    59, 64, 79, 80, 82–83, 86, 96,
    136–37
"Paddy's Pub: Home of the
    Original Kitten Mittens," 4, 22,
    65
paradigm, 163–64, 175
perception, 49, 52–53, 59, 96, 103

Peter John Olivi, 31, 33, 38, 39, 40
phenomenology, 65
philosophy, 19, 21, 25, 28–29, 103–110, 116, 128, 142
Plato, 4, 27, 104, 180
pleasure, 21–30, 57–58, 61–62, 80–82, 127
politics, 153
Popper, Karl, 160–62
principle, moral, 19, 24, 58, 80–81, 103–04, 114, 175, 195
psychoanalysis, 55–64, 130

rationality, 81, 104
rationalization, 51, 62
revenge, 11–12
revolutionary science, 163–64
"Reynolds vs. Reynolds: The Cereal Defense," 149–150, 159–160, 162, 165–66
Rickety Cricket, 24–25, 91, 98–101, 126, 129

science, 159–160, 162–66
selfishness, 17, 23, 57, 82, 87, 140, 142, 175, 179, 189–196
sex, 113–122
social norms, 45–52, 72–75
social responsibility, 16–19
sociopath, 113
soundness, 149
straw man fallacy, 155
suffering, 134
Sweet Dee; *see* Dee

"Sweet Dee Is Dating a Retarded Person," 117–18

truth, 37, 103, 145–177

Übermensch, 177–78
"Underage Drinking: A National Concern," 16, 82, 85, 87, 89, 115–16
unibrows, 48–50
utilitarianism, 136–142

validity, 149
value judgments, 75
"A Very Sunny Christmas," 5, 12, 15, 82, 124, 125, 198
violence, 7–8, 18–19
Virgin Mary, 31, 35
virtue, 80–88
virtue ethics, 80–88

the Waitress, 7, 11, 15, 28, 58, 67–68, 70, 74, 84–86, 91, 93–95, 106, 119, 124, 142, 161
"The Waitress Is Getting Married," 66, 93, 130
welfare, 3, 12, 25, 26, 68, 74, 82–83, 135, 144, 188, 192
"Who Got Dee Pregnant?" 14, 141
"Who Pooped the Bed?" 13, 70
wisdom, 22, 81, 92–93, 105, 109